Designer
Birdhouses

Designer
Birdhouses

20 Upscale Homes
for Sophisticated Birds

Richard T. Banks

LARK BOOKS

A Division of Sterling Publishing Co., Inc.
New York / London

Editor:
Larry Shea

Art Director:
Susan McBride

Cover Designer:
Cindy La Breacht

Art Production Assistance:
Jeff Hamilton

Editorial Assistance:
Mark Bloom, Cassie Moore,
Kathleen McCafferty,
and Amanda Wheeler

Project Photographers:
John Widman
Keith Wright (winter shots)

Technical Photographer:
Steve Mann

Illustrations:
Richard T. Banks

Illustration Text Production:
Orrin Lundgren

Proofreader:
Jessica Boing

Library of Congress Cataloging-in-Publication Data

Banks, Richard T., 1937-
  Designer birdhouses : 20 upscale homes for sophisticated birds
/ Richard T. Banks. -- 1st ed.
     p. cm.
  Includes index.
  ISBN-13: 978-1-57990-834-8 (pb-trade pbk. : alk. paper)
  ISBN-10: 1-57990-834-9 (pb-trade pbk. : alk. paper)
  1. Birdhouses--Design and construction. I. Title.
  QL676.5.B25 2008
  690'.8927--dc22

                          2007023933

10 9 8 7 6 5 4 3 2 1

First Edition

Published by Lark Books, A Division of
Sterling Publishing Co., Inc.
387 Park Avenue South, New York, N.Y. 10016

Text © 2008, Richard T. Banks
Photography © 2008, Lark Books
Illustrations © 2008, Richard T. Banks

Distributed in Canada by Sterling Publishing,
c/o Canadian Manda Group, 165 Dufferin Street
Toronto, Ontario, Canada M6K 3H6

Distributed in the United Kingdom by GMC Distribution Services,
Castle Place, 166 High Street, Lewes, East Sussex, England BN7 1XU

Distributed in Australia by Capricorn Link (Australia) Pty Ltd.,
P.O. Box 704, Windsor, NSW 2756 Australia

If you have questions or comments about this book,
please contact:
Lark Books
67 Broadway
Asheville, NC 28801
(828) 253-0467

Manufactured in China

ISBN 13: 978-1-57990-834-8
ISBN 10: 1-57990-834-9

For information about custom editions, special sales, premium and corporate purchases,
please contact Sterling Special Sales Department at 800-805-5489 or specialsales@sterlingpub.com.

Contents

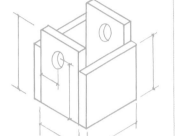

Introduction

'm not a bird expert—I'll leave that to the ornithologists. I'm an architect with a fondness for birds and a love for woodworking. Considering my background, it's not that big of a stretch to go from building for people to building for birds. To tell how that happened, I have to go back to a Christmas several years ago.

Each year I make my wife a special gift for Christmas and one for her birthday. The two events are close together, so coming up with new gift ideas can be a challenge. So there I was, a week before Christmas, without a clue of what to make for her. One morning, mindlessly gazing out the window at our garden, it hit me—"Why not a birdhouse?" It seemed like the perfect gift. My wife is an avid gardener who loves to "play in the dirt," and what better way to show my appreciation for her than with a gift for her garden. She loved her birdhouse, and the rest is history. Well, not quite.

As her garden grew, so did the number of birdhouses, and people began to take notice. Before I knew it, I was asked to make more birdhouses. Now the original ones were figments of my imagination; once made, they were difficult to duplicate. To keep up with the unexpected demand, I had to find a way to simplify my building process, while still creating birdhouses that were attractive and well-constructed. I came up with the idea of the "basic box"—a simple concept I'll use throughout this book. By varying this theme and adding embellishments, I was able to create a number of distinctive designs. This idea has worked so well that, with the help of my eldest son, a mom-and-pop Web birdhouse business was born: *www.architecturaleditions.com*.

While building birdhouses, I learned more about birds and their quest for survival. As an architect I am acutely aware of the damage done by poorly planned developments and unrelenting urban sprawl, and with it, the destruction of natural breeding habitats for cavity-nesting birds. I started my own crusade to encourage others to put up nest boxes for our feathered friends. The more I encouraged, the more I noticed what little the marketplace had to offer. Most birdhouses I saw were poorly designed, shoddily constructed, and wouldn't last a season. I became determined to show others how to design and build a better birdhouse, and the best way to do it was to write this book.

In the Basics section, we'll start with the tools, accessories, and building materials you'll need. We'll next move onto the essential theme of the book: creating the Basic Box and its variations. Then we'll have some fun talking about how to embellish the box and take it from the ordinary to something special.

In the Projects part of the book, I'll show you how to use the information in the previous section—along with just a little time and patience—to make a wide variety of birdhouse projects. You won't need to use any fancy tools or exotic woodworking techniques. You'll see some projects that kids can make, with just a little help from mom or dad. All the projects include diagrams, step-by-step instructions, and photographs of the completed birdhouses to help you visualize how they are made. You'll also find cutting lists along with lists of tools and materials to help you organize and obtain the items you'll need. Throughout the book, I'll include some information about bird habitats, nest box placement, and other fundamentals to keep your creation safe and healthy for birds, and useful for many years to come.

My hope is that you'll use this book not just to make a few lovely birdhouses, but also as a starting point for expanding your own design and technical skills. I'm reminded of something Walt Whitman once wrote: "It is not he who has done the best; it is he who suggests the most . . . who leaves you much to complete in your turn." I've written the book, and now it's your turn. I just know you can do it, and—best of all—have fun while you're at it.

The Basics

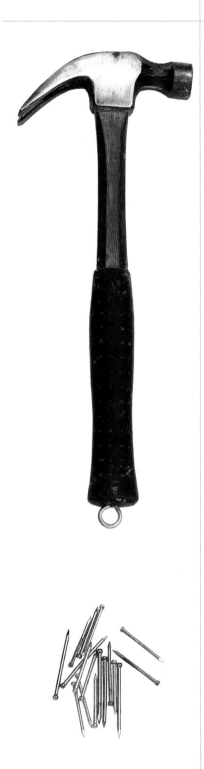

Basic Tools and Materials

Building a birdhouse is not exactly rocket science, and you don't need a workshop filled with expensive power tools and hard-to-find materials to be successful. The tools and related materials you'll need for making the birdhouses in this book fall into five basic categories by their functions—**measuring, cutting, drilling, fastening,** and **finishing.** We can also divide tools into two major categories—hand tools and power tools. Power tools can be further divided into handheld and stationary or bench tools.

For each function, I'll describe the different tools you have available to you. You can cut wood, for example, with a hand tool (such as a handsaw), a handheld power tool (a circular saw or jigsaw), or a variety of stationary or bench tools (a table saw, bandsaw, or scroll saw). The choice is up to you. You certainly can build these birdhouses with just hand tools, though there are some tasks that electrically powered tools will perform more quickly and efficiently. A handheld power drill, for example, is pretty close to an essential; you can use one to make birdhouse entry holes, drill air and drainage holes, make pilot holes for screws, and then drive those screws home with a screwdriver bit. And if you will be cutting many pieces of wood to different widths and at various angles, a table saw with a rip fence and miter gauge will save you time and effort.

That being said, I don't have a high-powered shop myself—just a few serviceable bench power tools like a table saw, bandsaw, drill press, and scroll saw. For assembly, I use a pneumatic nail gun that drives and countersinks a nail with a pull of the trigger. But don't get me wrong: I also depend on many of my trusty hand tools. Whatever tools you decide to employ, the important thing is to find the ones you are most comfortable with and that can do the job most efficiently. Above all, respect the tools you're using, and use them properly and safely. And have fun while you do!

Measuring

For measuring and layout work, a **tape measure** or **extention rule**, a **metal straightedge** or **ruler**, and a **carpenter's combination square** will help you do the job quickly and accurately. A combination square, especially the 16-inch-long version, is good for laying out cross-cut lines and 45° angles. For 60° angles, a simple 30°/60° **drafting triangle** will do.

From top: drafting triangle,
combination square,
extension rule, steel ruler

Cutting

For cutting wood, you have a wide range of tools to choose from. The best tool to pick will often depend on what tools you already own, your available shop space, and the task at hand.

Handheld Saws

For straight cuts, a standard **handsaw** will work fine. When you're cutting the small wooden pieces and narrow moldings that decorate many of these birdhouses, it's good to have a small **backsaw** and an aluminum **miter box**. They're great for making straight, even cuts, as well as the angled cuts needed to make corners come together neatly.

As far as electric handheld tools, a **circular saw** will make fast and straight cuts, and it can be adjusted to make bevel and miter cuts at various angles. Another versatile cutting tool is the handheld **electric jigsaw**. With the appropriate blade, it can make cuts in wood, metal, and plastic; cut curves, scrolls, and circles; and make pocket cuts (those cuts that make a hole in the middle of a piece) with or without a pilot hole. Jigsaws are also equipped with a guide that can be tilted for cutting miters and bevels.

From top: handsaw, backsaw, craft-type backsaw

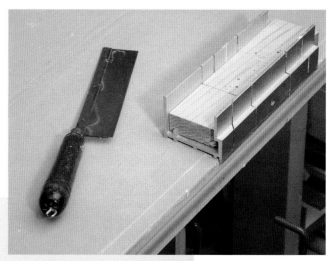

Small backsaw and aluminum miter box

Electric jigsaw

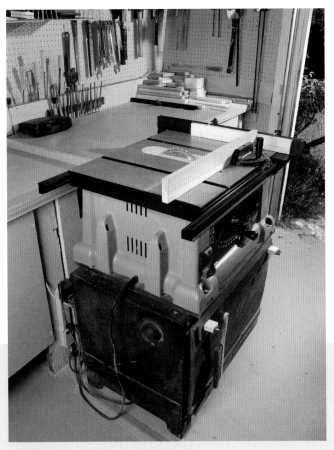

Table saw

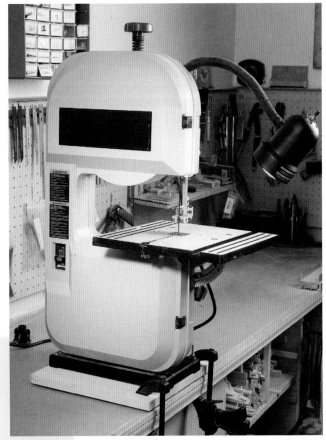

Bandsaw

Stationary and Bench Saws

If you have a **table saw**, I don't have to tell you about its speed, precision, and versatility. Another power saw that is helpful for many jobs, such as cutting small pieces or cutting along a curve, is the **bandsaw**. Bandsaws are also good for cutting thick pieces of wood, and they are less likely than table saws to have such problems as kickback, where a piece of wood is thrown back in the opposite of the cutting direction. For cutting finer curves, a good choice is a **scroll saw**. You can use its narrow blade to follow just about any delicate pattern.

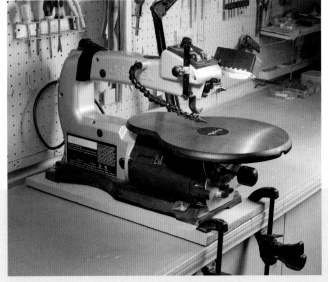

Scroll saw

Drilling

Drilling may be a more important task when making birdhouses than in just about any other type of woodworking. With birdhouses you actually *want* to leave holes in your work in order to allow the birds to get in, air to flow through, and water to drain out.

Electric Drills

The **hand drill**, either corded or cordless, is probably the one power tool found in more households than any other, and for good reason. With the proper accessories you can use it to drill pilot holes for other tools, fasten screws, cut out circles, and bore holes of various sizes. The most convenient type to use is one that is reversible, has variable speeds, and has a keyless chuck that makes it easy to remove and to tighten bits by hand.

Electric drill with screwdriver bits

A handheld drill can do any drilling task you'll need for building birdhouses. But if you also have a **drill press**, you'll find that it is a good choice for doing certain drilling jobs quickly and neatly.

Drill Bits

For all the tasks involved in building birdhouses, you'll need a variety of drill bits.

Twist drill bits, designed for drilling metal, are not the best for boring holes in wood. **Brad-point bits**, on the other hand, are modified twist drills with a sharp center point that keeps the bit from wandering and side spurs that cut wood fibers cleanly. For smaller-size holes in wood, these bits are excellent.

Spade bits are named for their flat, spade-like shape and come in a variety of sizes, including 1½ inches, an ideal diameter for most birdhouse entry holes. Holes cut with a spade bit can be rather rough, which is fine, as it makes for holes that are easier for birds to grip.

Forstner bits are designed with a near-full circular rim that allows them to cut very clean, straight holes through any grain direction and at any angle. Its short center spur and flat lower cutting edges leave a flat-bottomed hole that can be useful for creating decorative surface effects or seating dowels. They are not designed for boring through-holes.

Drill press

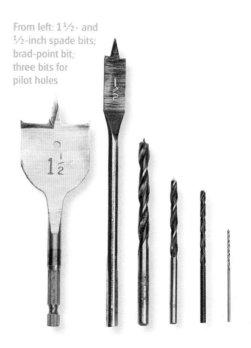

From left: 1½- and ½-inch spade bits; brad-point bit; three bits for pilot holes

Hole saws are a combination saw and drill bit; they're available in a wide range of diameters. As the name implies, hole saws have teeth like a saw and are useful for cutting holes with large diameters of up to several inches. With a multiple hole saw set, you can combine two cutters around the plunging bit and cut a donut-shaped wooden circle, something I use for a "predator guard" at the entry hole of my birdhouses.

Fastening

Once you've cut and drilled your pieces of wood, the following tools and materials will help you to put them together.

Clamps

Who couldn't use another set of hands? And that's exactly what clamps are, additional help in holding pieces steady when joining parts together. I find two varieties of clamps to be the handiest. One is the kind of throat clamp you close tight by squeezing a handle, and the other is the spring-loaded clamp. Both have the advantage of requiring only one free hand to put them into use. Other clamp varieties include the bar-type clamp and C-clamps, both of which you tighten by turning a part of the clamp attached to a threaded screw.

Bench hook

Bench Hooks

For a quick and easy method of assembly, without the aid of clamps or adhesive tape to hold pieces in place, I use a **bench hook** that I've made myself. It consists of a flat piece of medium-density fiberboard (MDF) with two 1 x 3-inch cleats attached to the top surface at a true 90° angle. A front cleat is attached to the underside of the MDF and acts as a hook, overlapping the top of your counter or workbench.

Screws and Screwdrivers

For fastening reliability, you can't beat screws. If your birdhouses will be exposed to weather (as they likely will), or if you're using redwood or cedar, **stainless steel screws** should be your choice. Above all, *don't* use drywall screws. Those flare-headed screws are designed for bearing against paper-faced drywall and don't have the strength of screws intended for fastening other materials.

There are four basic screw head types: **slot, Phillips, combo** or **square (Robertson)**. Of the four, square-headed screws are an excellent choice based on performance. With a square driverbit seated firmly in the screw head, you avoid head stripping and "spin out," and a lot of unnecessary aggravation.

From left: bar clamp, spring-loaded clamp, two sizes of squeeze clamps

From left: stainless steel and trim-head screws

The type of screw I prefer is a **trim-head screw**. It resembles a finishing nail but comes with a square slot in the top. The trumpet-shaped head and extremely sharp point allow this screw to countersink itself as it is being driven. It's a real time saver with strong holding power.

To drive screws, you'll need **screwdrivers** or **screwdriver bits** to match the specific screw head type you intend to use. To save time and labor, the easiest way to drive screws is with a screwdriver bit inserted in an electric drill. To keep wood from splitting and to make driving in screws easier and more precise, always drill pilot holes slightly smaller than the screw size you're using. You can do this with a narrow bit in an electric drill.

Nails

Nails, when used together with waterproof glue, are also an excellent fastening choice. There are over 100 varieties of nails you can buy. For birdhouse building, I think the best

At left, casing nails; at right, finishing nails

choice is the **casing nail**. These nails are a heavier version of the finishing nail, and have the same small head for countersinking with a nail set, leaving a hole to be filled prior to finishing. Filling holes makes for a little extra effort, but it prevents rust and it's good workmanship.

For attaching smaller pieces of wood to a birdhouse, such as strips of molding, a good choice is regular **finishing nails** or **brads**. These thinner nails are available in various lengths and thicknesses. When attaching narrow pieces of wood, be sure to choose a nail that is not so thick that it might split the wood as you drive it in.

Whatever size of nail you're using, the particular variety of nail to choose depends on its application. Left exposed, galvanized and other coated nails can be compromised by hammering. On the other hand, stainless steel's resistance to corrosion is uniform throughout. Again, if you're using redwood or western red cedar, you'll want to use stainless steel, as the tannic acid in the wood will cause unsightly staining with coated and galvanized nails.

In choosing the length of your nail or screw, a good rule of thumb is two to three times the thickness of the thinnest piece to be joined. For example, for nominal 1-inch lumber (¾-inch actual thickness), your nail or screw length would be between 1½ to 2 ¼ inches.

Hammers and Nail Guns

A regular-sized **hammer** works fine for most jobs, but it's also good to have a smaller one for the more delicate task of driving in smaller finishing nails and brads. Tapping carefully with a smaller hammer, you'll be less likely to hit your thumb as you start smaller nails—or at least it won't hurt quite so much if you do. Another handy tool to have when using finishing nails is a **nail set** to countersink the nail head below the surface.

Large and small hammers with nail set

As I mentioned earlier, I most often use a **pneumatic nail gun** that can drive and countersink a nail with one pull of a trigger. You don't need one to put together an occasional birdhouse, but if you do a fair amount of woodworking a nail gun is a great tool to have.

Pneumatic nail gun and nails

Glues and Adhesives

When screwing or nailing pieces together, you should apply glue first to ensure a strong joint. Choose a woodworking glue that is strong, waterproof, and can be easily sanded and painted.

To fasten small detailed pieces, you can use a lighter hammer with small brads, or else a **construction-grade adhesive**. These adhesives come in a form you can use with a caulking gun or in squeezable plastic containers. A good construction-grade adhesive is waterproof and fast-bonding with high strength, and it makes an excellent choice for fastening small wood or metal parts without the need for nails or screws.

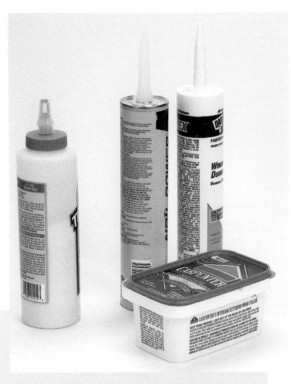

From left: wood glue, construction adhesive, acrylic latex caulk, wood filler

Finishing

For finishing birdhouses, the following tools and materials will make surfaces smooth and attractive.

Fillers and Caulks

For filling countersunk nail or screw holes in order to prevent rust and create a flat surface, I recommend using either a **carpenter's exterior wood filler**, or a type of **putty** you can mix with water to create a hard, durable filler.

For closing larger holes, gaps, or open joints, caulking is an elastic compound that does a great job. My preference is paintable **acrylic latex caulk** with silicone added for adhesion. You can buy it in a squeeze tube or a caulking-gun canister. Caulking acts as an adhesive bonding agent that seals water-suspect joints, particularly the ones on the roof and any other horizontal joint. It keeps water out and will extend the structural life of your nesting boxes. After your birdhouses have spent a few seasons out in the weather, caulking is very useful for touch up and maintenance.

Sandpaper and Sanding Blocks

Birdhouses don't really need a lot of sanding. A couple of grades of **garnet sandpaper** are about all you ever need to use: fine (180- to 150-grit), medium (120- to 80-grit) and coarse (60- to 50-grit). You can purchase a rubber sanding block to hold the paper, but it also works as well to wrap a piece of sandpaper around a dowel for circular sanding, or around a wood block for straight, flat work. I assure you, birds won't love you any more for a finely sanded box than for one that's just a little rough—they'll never know the difference.

From left: 100-, 150-, and 220-grit sandpaper; homemade sanding block; rubber sanding block

Paints and Finishes

In the Projects section of this book, you'll see the specific colors I've chosen to finish my birdhouses. When finishing your own creations, you can follow my suggestions, you can apply paint or stain to your own taste, or you can just leave your project natural, coated with wood sealer and a top coat of polyurethane for weather protection.

Whichever way you choose to go, it probably won't make much difference as far as attracting birds to your nesting box. Some people say that birds shy away from bright colors. According to the National Bird Feeding Society, however, the color of a birdhouse probably has little influence on birds choosing it. Proper dimensions of the entrance are more important.

When applying paint or stain for exterior exposure, the standard is a three-coat application—a base coat followed by two top coats. For paint, 100-percent acrylic latex has the ability to withstand every kind of weather condition, as it is more flexible and breathable than oil-based paints. I prefer a satin finish. If you decide to choose stain, I've found that solid stains tend to be more penetrating than transparent or semi-transparent varieties.

You'll need a brush about 2 inches wide for applying primer and basic top coats. You will also need some smaller artist's brushes if you want to create some of the designs or use the special painting techniques you'll see later in the book. Another big advantage of latex paint: it makes it much easier to clean up your brushes—and your hands—after painting, as you can use water and not mineral spirits.

Acrylic paints and an assortment of brushes

Tool Lists

What tools do you *really* need to make the birdhouses in this book? In the project instructions you'll see later, each list of required Tools and Accessories will refer you back to the following three lists.

The first few items in the Basic Tool Kit, from a handsaw to a screwdriver, really are essential. An electric jigsaw is good to have, and for projects that involve cutting curves, having one (or else a scroll saw) is necessary. With the layout and assembly tools later in the list, it's more a question of what tools you have available and what methods you want to use.

The Power Shop Tools are described within the projects as "optional" because you can do just about everything you need to without them. When one of these tools can do a particular step in a project more easily or efficiently than other tools, I'll let you know. And the Safety Essentials, along with good safety practices, are just what they say they are—essential.

Basic Tool Kit

Handsaw

Hammer

Nail set

Electric drill with drill bits

Screwdriver

Handheld electric jigsaw

Craft-type backsaw and miter box

Carpenter's combination square

Drafting triangles, 45° and 30°/60°

Metal ruler or straightedge

Tape measure

Assorted clamps

Bench hook

Power Shop Tools

Table saw

Scroll saw

Bandsaw

Drill press

Safety Essentials

Safety goggles

Work gloves

Dust mask

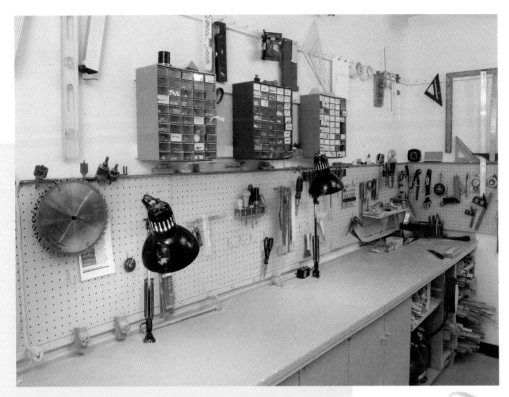

Setting Up Shop and Working Safely

Now that we've covered the basic hand tools you'll need, and some power tools to make work easier and faster, let's say a few words about arranging a safe and efficient workspace.

My shop is quite simple, measuring 10 feet wide by 14 feet long with a center aisle and counters on each side. Other than my base-mounted table saw, my bench power tools sit on the counter, mounted on wooden bases for mobility. When I need it, I just slide a power tool down the counter and clamp it in place at a convenient location. My hand tools and accessories are hung off the wall or stored on shelves, with my portable power tools tucked away below the counter.

Do you need a shop like this to successfully build a few birdhouses? Certainly not. But you will require a place to work. The place you choose should be clean and uncluttered, away from other activities, especially food preparation areas. You should have grounded power outlets for any corded electrical tools you use and adequate counter space for layout, measuring, and assembly. All your tools and equipment should be chosen ahead of time, placed well at hand and within easy reach. Above all, make sure you have excellent lighting conditions, whether it is overhead or task lighting.

Dust mask, safety goggles, and work gloves

Whatever space you work in and whatever tools you choose, safety should always be your first and foremost consideration. Here are some guidelines to follow:

■ Dress properly: don't wear loose clothing or jewelry that can get caught up in moving parts.

■ Wear **safety goggles** and a **dust mask** whenever you're cutting or drilling pieces that could create chips, splinters, or a lot of sawdust.

■ If you use loud power tools, like a table saw, use **ear protection**.

■ Keep your work area clean and well-swept, with no loose electrical cords, so that you won't slip or trip.

■ Have a **first-aid kit** handy, and a **phone** nearby for emergencies.

It all comes down to a combination of common sense and alertness. If you're doing something that looks and feels wrong, it probably is. Woodworking is a hobby that involves sharp objects, often spinning at high speeds. The possible cost of making a mistake is so great that you should take every precaution you can.

Wood for Birdhouses

Wood is the primary material used for all the projects in this book. Particular projects will require that you buy a few other inexpensive and easy-to-find materials; we'll discuss those later in the section "From Basic to Not-So-Basic."

You can make nesting boxes from a variety of materials, but wood is still king. It's a good insulator under hot or cold conditions, readily available, easily worked with hand or power tools, and akin to a bird's natural habitat. However, wood does have its shortcomings. Being a natural material, it absorbs and releases moisture which can lead to distortion. The art of working with wood is to anticipate changes in moisture to minimize dimensional changes. Surface coatings are one defense, but no coating is entirely moisture proof. To get the most out of wood, you have to take care in selecting, storing, and working with it.

Selecting Lumber

How a board is sawed from a log also affects its stability. Boards from your local lumberyard or home improvement store are generally plain-sawn. This results in grain lines at the board end that run the width of the board. Even though the boards are kiln-dried, they still have a tendency to swell, shrink, cup, and twist. If possible, try to purchase quarter-sawn boards, in which short grain lines run vertically at the end of the board. Also seek out tight-grained boards instead of wide-grained, as they're less prone to cupping and warping.

Lumber is graded according to its surface appearance and thickness. For birdhouse construction you will be using boards—that is, lumber that is less than 2 inches thick and is graded on a diminishing scale based on surface imperfections. You should choose from Select C grade to No. 1 Common or even the lower-quality (and less expensive) No. 3 Common. Don't buy the most expensive boards available. For one thing, if you're finishing your birdhouses with paint or a solid stain, imperfections in the wood won't be apparent.

Sizes of Lumber

When selecting boards and strips of lumber, remember that they are sold according to their **nominal dimension**. The actual size is the dimension that comes from the mill after the piece is surfaced. For example, a standard 2 x 4 is actually 1½ inches by 3½ inches. The following chart is a handy reference for selecting the right board size.

Standard Dimensions of Softwood Boards in Inches

Nominal Size	Actual Size
1 x 1	¾ x ¾
1 x 2	¾ x 1½
1 x 4	¾ x 3½
1 x 6	¾ x 5½
1 x 8	¾ x 7¼
1 x 10	¾ x 9¼
1 x 12	¾ x 11¼

Another handy lumber dimension is the standard 4 x 4. It actually measures 3 ½ inches by 3 ½ inches and is suitable for mounting all the projects in this book.

In The Projects section, I've included cutting lists, indicating the board sizes you'll need in order to make the fewest cuts with the least waste.

Varieties of Wood

In North America, the principal soft-woods used for making nesting boxes are pine, cedar, cypress, Douglas fir, redwood, and poplar (although poplar is technically a hardwood). Each species has different characteristics. Some are dimensionally more stable and better at resisting rot and insect damage. And you'll find a lot of variability regarding cost and availability.

Pine

Pine is readily available, economical, and the most common wood available at your local home improvement store. Pine is easy to work, lightweight, and soft. It holds paint well and is a good choice for nesting boxes, even though it's prone to warping.

Top, from left to right: pine, cedar, and poplar boards; at bottom, trim board

Cedar

Among the six common species of cedar, Western Red Cedar is the most popular for birdhouses. It is native to the northwestern United States, strong, lightweight, easy to work, and has very low shrinkage. It also holds paint well and is highly resistant to decay, but it can be expensive and has a tendency to split and splinter. Like redwood, cedar bleeds tannins, which can appear as dark stains around fasteners and even show through paint.

Cypress

Cypress is primarily found in the southeast United States. It's not easy to find, is difficult to nail, and exhibits decay pockets known as pecks. However, it is highly resistant to decay, exhibits moderate shrinkage, and holds paint well.

Douglas Fir

Grown in the Pacific Northwest, Douglas fir is a strong, hard, heavy wood that holds paint extremely well and is moderately priced, but not readily available outside of the region where it is grown.

Redwood

Like Douglas fir, redwood is primarily grown in the Pacific coast region. It's a straight-grain wood that is easily worked, holds paint well, shrinks very little, and is highly resistant to decay. It is relatively expensive, though, and has a tendency to split and crack. Redwood also has the same problems with tannins as Western Red Cedar.

Poplar

Poplar is sometimes referred to as the "soft hardwood." It is light to medium in weight, strong, soft, and easily worked. It is moderately priced and grown primarily in the eastern United States. With its very close grain, it is an excellent choice for detail work and moldings.

Treated Wood

Don't use chemically treated arsenical wood—with labels such as CCA, ACA, and ACZA—in your birdhouse construction. These wood products can be hazardous to your health and that of your feathered friends. The most common chemical treatment, CCA (chromate copper arsenate), was recently replaced with ACQ (alkaline copper quat). ACQ is much safer to use, holds up well under outdoor conditions, and won't make a tasty lunch for insects.

Stickered stack of pine boards

Storing Wood

The lumber you buy is usually kiln-dried. However it's good practice to allow any excess moisture to escape and to keep the wood from getting damp. As shown in the photo above, I "sticker" the boards I'm planning to use by stacking them with wood scraps between them. This allows air to circulate around the wood and prevents any buildup of moisture.

Plywood and Other Flat Materials

Plywood is a manufactured product made up of glued-together layers of wood. This makes for joints that are difficult to create, and edges that require special attention to prevent them from delaminating. If you use plywood, make sure the kind you choose is for exterior use or marine grade.

I also use **trim board**. It's a hardboard wood product made from 100-percent wood fiber coated with protective resins and finished with an oven-cured primer. I use it primarily for birdhouse roofs. It serves as a good base for supporting lattice or other materials, or used alone as an exposed roof. However, any visible underside of the material must be sealed, and the top surface finished with two coats of durable paint. Trim board is thinner than wood, tends to be brittle, and is not suitable for Basic Box construction.

Building the Basic Box

f you build it, will they come? When it comes to birdhouses, the answer is not necessarily. If you build a nesting box for the wrong species in the wrong environment, they won't. In North America, of the 920 known birds, only 85 are classified as primary or secondary cavity-nesters. Primary nesters make their own nesting holes with each new breeding season. Secondary cavity-nesters aren't so lucky. They depend on hollows made by other birds, crevices found in decaying trees, or man-made nesting boxes. Of this group approximately 50 species will regularly inhabit birdhouses. It sounds like a small number, but the sheer volume of these birds and the steady decline in suitable nesting places is what makes building birdhouses so essential to their survival.

So what makes a good birdhouse? The answer is quite simple:

▓ Adequate box and entry-hole size for the intended species.

▓ Solid construction for weather-tightness and durability.

▓ Security for warding off predators.

Birdhouse Dimensions

Birdhouses do not have to be mathematically precise. The *Birdhouse Data and Dimensions* chart—organized according to nest box size—shows that small cavity-nesters can be accommodated in boxes of similar dimensions. The same holds true for larger birds. Entry holes of 1½ inches in diameter will suffice for all small birds and still keep aggressive starlings at bay. For larger birds, entry holes tend to be more species-specific.

These nesting box dimensions are useful guidelines, but knowing something about a bird's dominant habitat is more important. You wouldn't build a nesting box to attract a particular bird without knowing where that bird is likely to live and breed. The alphabetical key to the chart will give you an idea of the dominant habitats associated with particular species.

The chart to the right is only a basic guide. After all, birds are creatures in the wild, and they don't go about measuring holes or potential nesting boxes. All the birdhouses in this book fall within basic parameters that will accommodate all small-cavity nesting birds and some larger birds as well. With an emphasis on attracting small birds, most projects here start as a Basic Box with a floor measuring 4 to 5 inches square; an interior height of 6 to 12 inches; and an entry hole 1½ inches in diameter, located 5 to 8 inches above the floor.

In this section, I'll go through the steps needed to create a typical Basic Box. I'll also give you some tips on cutting, drilling, and creating different types of joints. You'll then be prepared to build the projects later in the book; they are all based on the Basic Box and its variations.

Chart Key

A = Forest edges, meadows, open woods, groves, golf courses, and parks

B = Wooded open forests, farmlands, mixed coniferous and deciduous trees

C = Pastures, fields, meadows, parks, and woodlots

D = Open fields with scattered trees

E = Open fields near water, pastures, and marshes

F = Dry plains spotted with trees or cacti; semi-desert

G = Forest edges, shallow water, mixed deciduous or coniferous trees

H = Open forests, fresh water, marshes, and swamps

I = Lakes, rivers, and ponds; mudflats

J = Areas of scrub vegetation, frequently with thorn bushes

Birdhouse Data & Dimensions

Bird	Floor Size	Entrance Hole Diameter	Hole Height Above Floor	Interior Height	Height Above Ground (in feet)	Dominant Habitat
Downy Woodpecker	3 x 3 – 4 x 4	1¼ – 1½	8 – 12	8 – 10	5 – 20	G
Black-capped Chickadee	4 x 4 – 5 x 5	1⅛ – 1½	6 – 8	8 – 12	5 – 15	A
Carolina Chickadee	4 x 4 – 5 x 5	1⅛ – 1½	6 – 8	8 – 12	5 – 15	A
Mountain Chickadee	4 x 4 – 5 x 5	1⅛ – 1½	6 – 8	8 – 12	5 – 15	A
Brown-headed Nuthatch	4 x 4 – 5 x 5	1⅛ – 1½	6 – 7	9 – 12	5 – 15	B
White-breasted Nuthatch	4 x 4 – 5 x 5	1⅛ – 1½	6 – 8	8 – 12	5 – 20	A
House Finch	4 x 4 – 5 x 5	1½	4 – 7	9 – 12	5 – 15	J
Bewick's Wren	4 x 4 – 5 x 5	1¼ – 1½	4 – 7	9 – 12	5 – 10	B
Carolina Wren	4 x 4 – 5 x 5	1 – 1½	4 – 7	6 – 12	5 – 10	B
House Wren	4 x 4 – 5 x 5	1 – 1½	4 – 7	6 – 12	5 – 10	C
Plain Titmouse	4 x 4 – 5 x 5	1⅜ – 1½	6 – 7	9 – 12	5 – 15	B
Tufted Titmouse	4 x 4 – 5 x 5	1⅜ – 1½	6 – 7	8 – 12	5 – 15	B
Tree Swallow	4 x 4 – 5 x 5	1¼ – 1½	4 – 6	9 – 12	5 – 15	E
Violet-green Swallow	4 x 4 – 5 x 5	1¼ – 1½	4 – 6	6 – 12	5 – 15	E
Prothonotary Warbler	4 x 4 – 5 x 5	1¼ – 1½	4 – 7	8 – 12	4 – 12	E
Eastern Bluebird	5 x 5	1½	6 – 7	8 – 12	5 – 10	A
Western Bluebird	5 x 5	1½	6 – 7	8 – 12	5 – 10	B
Mountain Bluebird	5 x 5	1½	6 – 7	8 – 12	5 – 10	B
Ash-throated Flycatcher	5 x 5 – 6 x 6	1½	6 – 7	8 – 12	3 – 20	F
Great-crested Flycatcher	5 x 5 – 6 x 6	1½	6 – 8	8 – 12	6 – 50	B
Golden-fronted Woodpecker	5 x 5 – 6 x 6	2	10 – 14	14 – 16	3 – 25	B
Red-headed Woodpecker	5 x 5 – 6 x 6	2	10 – 14	14 – 16	8 – 80	A
Purple Martin	6 x 6	2¼	1	6	5 – 20	E
Bufflehead Duck	6 x 6 – 7 x 7	2 – 3	17 – 19	16 – 24	6 – 20	I
Northern Flicker	6 x 6 – 8 x 8	2½	10 – 20	16 – 24	6 – 20	B
Screech Owl	8 x 8	3	10 – 12	12 – 18	6 – 20	D
American Kestrel	8 x 8 – 9 x 9	3	10 – 12	16 – 18	6 – 30	A
Common Goldeneye	10 x 10 – 12 x 12	3 x 4	16 – 18	24 – 25	6 – 30	I
Hooded Merganser	10 x 10 – 12 x 12	3 x 4	16 – 18	24 – 25	6 – 30	J
Wood Duck	10 x 10 – 12 x 12	3 x 4	16 – 18	24 – 25	6 – 30	H
Common Merganser	10 x 10 – 12 x 12	3 x 4	16 – 18	24 – 25	6 –30	A

NOTES:

▪ All dimensions are in inches unless noted.

▪ House sparrows and starlings are not listed because they are imported, aggressive species, and competitors with native nesting-box birds. As these birds were introduced from Europe, they are not protected by U.S. law and may be removed from nesting boxes.

Cutting Basics

When ripping a board lengthwise to the right width, or crosscutting perpendicular to the grain, use the guide on your portable saw. If you're cutting with a handsaw, clamp a straight-edged board to your work to guide your cut. Freehand cutting is not safe, and it yields poor results. If the board you're starting out with is too long, cut it at some convenient spot to make your work easier and safer.

Here are some more tips for cutting wood:

▧ Tape two matching pieces (like gables) together, and cut both in one operation. For small repetitive pieces, you can similarly tape strips together and cut several at one time.

▧ If you need duplicate pieces, cut one exactly to size and use it as a tracing guide for any additional pieces.

▧ Plastic templates and iron-on transfers can help to mark the lines for cutting standardized pieces.

▧ When you're cutting pieces to length and width, make all miter and bevel cuts at the same time. It saves time and effort later on.

If you're using a table saw, the same ideas apply, and these additional tips will add to your efficiency and safety:

▧ When ripping boards, use an auxiliary fence to prevent kickback.

▧ Use a miter gauge for straight crosscuts, and set it to the proper degree for angular cuts, using a stop block.

▧ Small duplicate pieces are easy to make with a stop block clamped to the bench top, allowing each piece to swing free as you cut it.

Ripping a board

Crosscutting a board

ANOTHER TIP

After you cut your required pieces, label them by writing on a piece of masking tape and sticking it on the workpiece. It also helps to include an arrow showing the proper assembly direction. Don't write on the wood, as you're just making extra work for yourself when it comes time to remove the marks.

Drilling Basics

You'll need several holes in each Basic Box, and it's best to drill them right after you cut your box pieces. Here are some tips and advice for drilling:

1 Small entry holes, 1½ inches in diameter, are best made with a spade bit by simply drilling partway through the wood until the point exits the opposite side. Turn the piece over and drill from the opposite side to complete the hole. This method makes drilling entry holes a lot easier and prevents the wood from ripping out.

2 To avoid drowning newly hatched nestlings, you'll need to use a pilot bit to drill ¼-inch drain holes in the bottom piece of the box, preferably one in each corner. As an option, when using a recessed bottom, you can cut all four corners on a slight angle for the same purpose.

3 A pilot bit can also be used for drilling ventilation holes. These should be located higher rather than lower, and across from one another, in order to release the upward flow of heat. Another ventilation method I find useful, when the design allows it, is to cut the sides lower than the front and back to create an air slot for cross ventilation.

4 When setting round columns, it's a good idea to seat them in a flat bottom hole made with a Forstner bit to protect the exposed end grain and to provide for proper vertical alignment.

5 Creating pilot holes is always your best option when driving screws, and they can also help when starting larger holes. Large oval-shaped holes can be cut by first drilling a pilot hole and then proceeding to cut the oval with a jigsaw. Any interior or pocket hole can be cut in a wood surface using the same starter-hole method.

6 Drill all your holes prior to assembly, including pilot holes for screws.

And lastly, when you're drilling through-holes, be sure to place a scrap piece of sacrificed wood under your workpiece. This will help keep your piece from splitting and splintering—and it also might help keep your workbench or counter from being filled with holes.

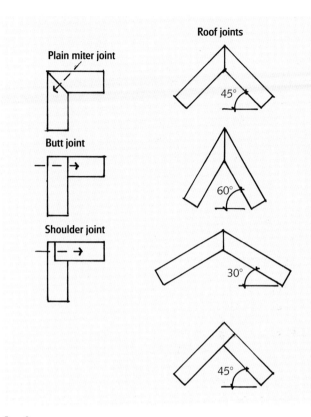

Joints

For durability and water-tightness, solid joints are your first line of defense. In nest box building, the three most basic joints are the **plain miter**, **butt**, and **shoulder joint**. For the 90° angles of the sides of the Basic Box, an accurately cut and well-fastened butt joint will work just fine.

Roofs are a little trickier. The miter joint is generally the best choice for sloped roofs because it doesn't expose vulnerable end grain. A butt joint is easier to create for a roof, particularly for 45° slopes, but to survive harsh weather conditions it will require some end-grain treatment. Shoulder joints fit somewhere between the other two types for strength and end-grain protection, but because of the extra work they take, I don't use them in birdhouse construction.

A more difficult roof joint to make is the 60° gable miter. Even a bench saw isn't much help without some kind of a jig, as most saw blades cannot be tilted to a 60° angle. However, if you don't mind dealing with end grain, a compromised 60° joint can be made by cutting two boards at a 30° bevel and joining them in what might be termed a butt-miter joint, as shown on page 62.

Let's face it: woodworking joints all have their pros and cons, and it comes down to choices and compromises that you must make. Nonetheless, any joint that exposes end grain is a problem joint and needs to be properly sealed with one of these methods:

▨ Prior to painting, coat the exposed grain with a mixture of two parts waterproof glue to one part water.

▨ Spread a thin coat of paintable caulking adhesive over the grain.

▨ Paint two coats of clear acrylic medium over the exposed joint—one coat before painting and one coat after.

You should also pay close attention to all joints located in horizontal surfaces; caulk them or use one of the suggested sealing methods. There is also an old construction rule of thumb that says: if a water-suspect joint points its nose to the sky—caulk it!

An Important Safety Note!

The photographs in this book sometimes include power tools being used without their safety guards attached. This is done to show the processes more clearly and is not a recommended practice. You should be sure to follow all directions that come with your power tools and to use all applicable safety features.

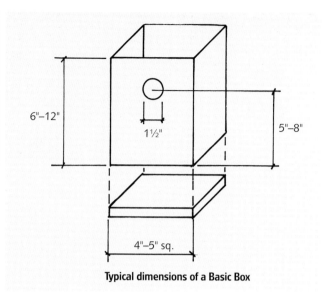

Typical dimensions of a Basic Box

Cutting Pieces for the Basic Box

Now let's apply the building basics to a practical situation and make a Basic Box.

In the accompanying photos, I'll be showing you how to cut the pieces for a Basic Box on a table saw, but the principles of measuring and cutting will work no matter what kind of saw you use. Cutting a board to length and width is a job that a handsaw can also handle quickly and easily.

Most Basic Boxes you'll see in this book will have two identical fronts and two identical side pieces. The diagrams that accompany each project will give you the correct dimensions for each piece. Here's how to lay out and cut a typical Basic Box component to the right size.

A

B

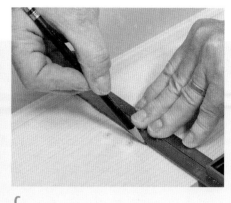

C

1 Set a combination square to the desired width of your piece, hold the square against the side of the board you'll be cutting, and mark the distance with a pencil (photo A). You can use a ruler or a tape measure to make these measurements instead, but a combination square makes it easier to draw accurate lines at perfect 90° angles.

2 Reset the square to the desired length of the piece, move it to the end of the board, and mark that distance from the end (photo B). You'll then use the square (or a ruler) to draw a line where the board will be crosscut (photo C).

3 With the saw of your choice, rip the board along the pencil line to the desired width. On the table saw, you do this by setting the rip fence to the correct width, and pushing the board through (photo D). (For safety, use a pushstick to push the far end of the board past the blade.) If you're using a handheld saw, clamp a straight board onto the board you're cutting to guide your saw.

4 Crosscut the board to the desired length. On a table saw, your miter gauge will ensure a 90° cut (photo E). If you're cutting by hand, you can again clamp a straight board to guide your saw.

D

E

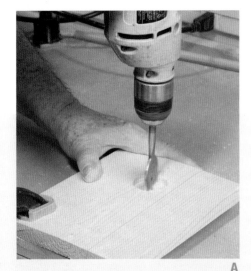

A

B

C

Drilling Holes in the Basic Box

After you've cut out all four pieces for the Basic Box and before you put them together, it's time to drill some holes.

1 Measure and mark the center point of the bird entry hole on the front piece(s) of the box. Clamp the piece onto a scrap piece of wood on your bench or counter. Then drill through the wood with a spade bit (photo A).

2 If your birdhouse design requires holes for ventilation, measure and mark the spots on the side pieces for them. Then use a ½-inch brad-point or spade bit to drill through your marks (photo B).

3 If you're assembling the box with screws instead of nails, now's the time to drill pilot holes. Mark where each screw will go, and use a drill bit a little narrower than your screws to make the pilot holes (photo C).

Assembling the Basic Box

You've got four sides of a box, cut and drilled. Before you assemble your nest box, spend a little time in preparation.

▦ Clean all debris from the surfaces to be joined—sawdust, wood chips, or splinters.

▦ Make sure all exposed surfaces have been properly sealed.

▦ For good measure, temporarily tape your pieces together to check for proper fit, accurate joints, or any uneven surfaces that you may regret later.

There are several ways to assemble the Basic Box. You can hold the pieces together with clamps or tape while you drive your fasteners, or you can use a simple bench hook for alignment and support. You can also use screws or nails, along with glue. I'll explain just about every way you can do it.

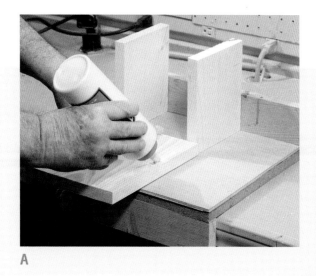

A

B

C

Whatever method you use to put together the box, you'll need to first apply a bead of glue to the inside edges of the front piece where they'll meet the sides (photo A). A thinner coat is better than a thicker one. After you've applied the glue, use one of the following methods for assembly:

1 *If you're using a bench hook and screws:* Arrange the front and two sides of the box in the bench hook. Drive the screws through the pilot holes, pressing the pieces against the back cleat of the bench hook for support and alignment (photo B). After you've attached the front, turn the piece around and screw on the back in the same way. Overall, this is probably the easiest method.

2 *If you're using a bench hook and nails:* Set up the side pieces with the front piece on top, and nail the top piece on (photo C). Drive your nails at a slight angle (varying angles from nail to nail), and they will be less likely to pull out over time. A bench hook is great for keeping pieces aligned, but you could do this step just on the bench top if you don't have one. After you've nailed on the front, flip the box parts over and repeat this step with the back.

3 *If you're using clamps and screws:* Clamp together the four pieces in the correct alignment. Drive the screws into the pilot holes (photo D). Here I'm using a screwdriver instead of an electric drill and screwdriver bit—either works fine.

TIP

Dipping your nail or screw in butcher's wax or sticking it into a bar of soap before you drive it helps it go in easier.

D

Bases

I usually consider the base, or bottom of the box, as separate from the box itself. My favored means of attachment is from the underside, allowing the base to serve as a nesting platform, a means of access for you to clean out the box, and a mounting device all in one. Regardless of how a base is cut, the ones you'll create in this book all share common features: concealed rust-resistant fasteners; protection from water intrusion; and four blocks, or feet, for interior display. The following bases are the ones most generally used:

- The chamfer, with its beveled edges and ¼-inch recess

- Square cut, featuring a ¼-inch setback

- Semi-recessed, with one surface concealed and the other set back

- The flat plate: a basic block attached to the underside of a pocket hole

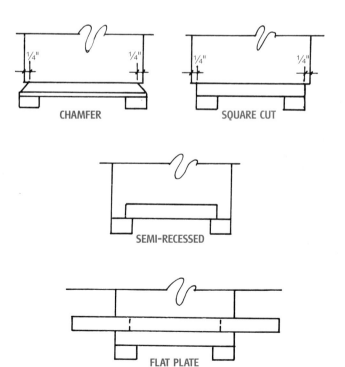

CHAMFER

SQUARE CUT

SEMI-RECESSED

FLAT PLATE

Basic Box Variations

A Basic Box can be tall, short, narrow, or wide and still be a captivating nesting place for birds. I've developed four variations of the Basic Box that serve as the underlying structure for all the designs you'll see in this book. Each project begins with one of these variations, which should help you to visualize a particular design and understand its simple origin.

Variation 1 is a rectilinear box composed of straight-cut pieces. It's the kind we made in this chapter, and you can use it with added gables of varying designs.

Variation 2 is the integral gable box, with slopes of 30º, 45º, or 60º on the front and back pieces that create the basic roof line.

Variation 3 is composed of either a rectilinear or a gable-type box, but crowned with a special top—a cantilevered platform, pyramid, or plateau.

Variation 4 is what I refer to as the "three-sided box." Technically this form is not really a box but more of a nesting pocket. However, when attached to a freeform front and back, the assembly creates not only a box, but one that can be quite unique and playful.

So where do we go from here? Well, if you were to take any of these Basic Box variations with an adequate entry hole, then attach a top and bottom, you might attract a bird or two. But the end result might not be the most fascinating feast for the human eye. Luckily, this is but the beginning. From here on the real fun begins, as we start with these basic forms and add design ideas, embellishments, decoration, and more. The best is yet to come!

30°

45°

60°

From Basic to Not-So-Basic

If **variety is the spice of life,** birdhouses have to be one of the better seasonings. They can be found in a vast array of shapes, sizes, and colors, and made from every imaginable material you can think of, including some you may have never thought possible. Birdhouses can be purely functional, fanciful, or downright bizarre, but one thing is for sure: they offer a great opportunity for artistic expression and personal gratification. Building birdhouses can be fun for the whole family—a great way to teach the little ones about art and design while showing them how to handle and respect tools.

So where do you start? Like the projects in this book, you start from the basics and progress to the not-so-basic, trying your hand at the projects that interest you the most and are best suited to your skill level. Regardless of where you start, it all begins with one of the Basic Boxes. Change a few shapes, alter a few features, embellish a surface or two, add some of your own creative juices, and you will have a recipe for success.

In this part of the book I will show you how to begin changing a simple box into a fascinating birdhouse by changing shapes; altering features; and working with slopes, special tops, and freeform designs. I'll introduce you to the concept of surface embellishment, using products purchased off the shelf and ones you can make. We will explore such subjects as security features, templates, and finishing and installing your birdhouse. Everything here comes together and is put to use in the Projects section that follows.

Changing Shapes
and Altering Features

I mentioned earlier that the birdhouses in this book all start out as one of four variations on the Basic Box. Now let's see how four variations can turn into an essentially limitless number of designs.

Take a simple box (**Variation 1**) and attach a dominant design element, like a prominent gable to support the roof, and you can transform a Basic Box so it no longer resembles its humble beginnings. You can alter this feature by cutting it in half, adding columns, or extending legs—all using the design theme of the enlarged gable.

A standard feature like an added gable can also be transformed by simply cutting different geometric shapes within the same feature—a circle, triangle, or square. In addition, by changing colors and adding patterns, what started out as a common feature can end up yielding designs that are quite distinct and different.

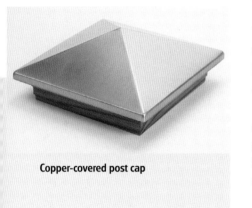

Copper-covered post cap

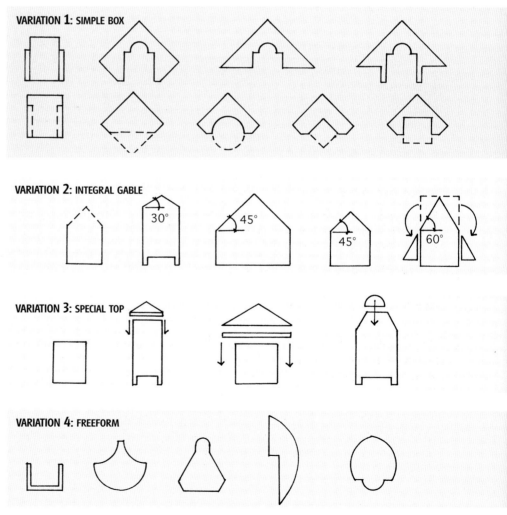

A box with integral gables (**Variation 2**) offers many opportunities for changing features and shapes. I use 30º, 45º, and 60º slopes since they are the easiest to cut and the simplest to reproduce. To add variety, you can change the height, expand the width, cut some legs in the basic form, and re-use pieces that are often discarded to create a whole new shape.

Adding a special top (**Variation 3**) is usually eye-catching, and another way to transform a basic rectangular box into a sophisticated artistic statement. One simple topping device is a standard large-size post cap (6 inches square). You can buy it right off the shelf in any home improvement store. A cantilevered wood platform is another useful feature that adds dimension to a box and provides for added gables for additional variety.

For endless variety, and I do mean endless, you can't beat the freeform shape. Four projects in this book illustrate the potential of adding free-form shapes to what I call the three-sided box (**Variation 4**)—a bottom with two sides. You can easily duplicate these shapes by using the small-scale templates I've provided.

Templates

For making some of the projects, not just those with freeform shapes, templates are not only useful but necessary. In laying out a more complicated gable design, I suggest using polyester film or standard stencil material with the design cut to the exact shape and size for easy tracing. For simple integral gables of 30º, 45º, or 60º, you won't need a template. The best method is to join two pieces together, draw the proper slope on one piece, and cut the pieces in one operation.

Freeform shapes and some decorative designs (like those used for decoupage and stenciling) may require that you mechanically enlarge small-scale drawings to form paper or cardstock cut-outs. The best way is to enlarge the drawing at your local copy center. If you are making only one or two birdhouses, basic templates of paper or cardstock will work just fine. However, for stencil designs you will need standard stenciling material or polyester film for cutting your stencils.

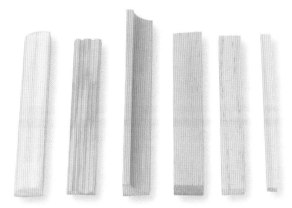
Wooden moldings, from left: shoe, screen, cove, two rectangular and one square

Decorative and Other Added Elements

Each birdhouse in this book starts out as a wooden box. To decorate and embellish these plain boxes, you'll be using some premade pieces you can buy at your local home improvement store and others you can make yourself.

Moldings, Trim, and Other Wooden Items

Moldings are usually sold in 8-foot lengths and can be conveniently cut to size using a small backsaw and miter box. If you have a table saw, you can create strip moldings from wood stock.

A variety of wooden pieces are also available in different sizes and shapes at home improvement and craft stores. Some pieces—like balls, half balls, and wood buttons—can be used as is and fastened with glue and small finishing nails, using a predrilled pilot hole to avoid splitting. Other wooden pieces, such as dowels, will need to be cut to the right length or size.

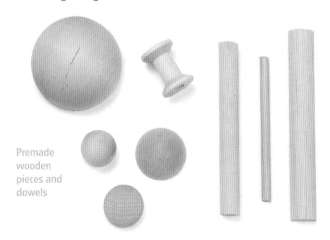
Premade wooden pieces and dowels

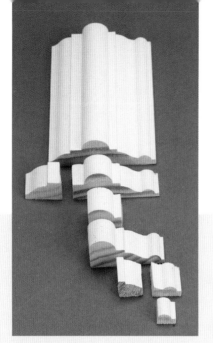

Chair rail molding cut to various profiles

#6

3"

#3

1"

#1

5/8"

#4

2"

#7

2 3/8"

1/2"

#2

1"

#5

3/4"

Chair Rail Molding

Now this type of molding is a real find. As the photo and illustrations indicate, you can cut a variety of sizes and shapes from a standard chair rail molding found at any home improvement store. This technique serves as a great shortcut for making special curved shapes for column capitals, brackets, or other adornments. I've numbered each profile piece from #1 through #7 to correspond to a particular shape that is used for different projects. Some numbers you see in the Projects section will be references to this diagram.

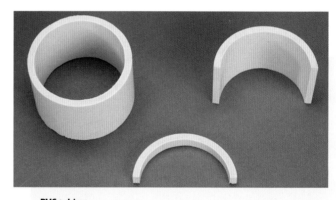

PVC tubing

PVC Tubing

PVC tubes come in a variety of sizes, but I prefer the 3 ½-inch diameter by ¼-inch thick size for use with birdhouses. You can cut them with a hack saw, table saw, bandsaw, or even a standard backsaw. Half pieces are useful for roof shapes, and round segments work well as entry-hole predator guards. If the edges are rough after cutting, a little sandpaper will smooth them out. To adhere PVC to just about any surface, construction adhesive is best. Finishing nails and glue work as well, though I suggest you predrill small pilot holes before nailing.

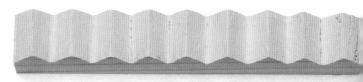

Hardware

Other than nails and screws to keep them together, birdhouses don't require a lot of hardware. A few items that you may need for the projects are hinges or hooks to allow the birdhouse to be opened or to keep it closed.

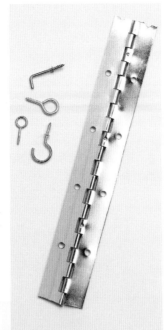

Hooks and a hinge

It's not too difficult to make your own moldings; the photos on this page show four that you can fabricate without too much trouble. Though basic, they do require an accurate layout and some patience. Ideally you should make a plastic template, and cut precisely for multiple strips, though you can also measure and set your cut lines directly on the wood strip.

The four moldings shown here, labeled M1 through M4, have the following dimensions:

- **M1:** a ⅛-inch-wide saw cut is made on the top edge of the molding every ½ inch to a depth of ¼ inch

- **M2:** 45° notches are cut every ¾ inch to ⅜ inch deep

- **M3:** 45° notches are cut every ½ inch to ¼ inch deep

- **M4:** a ⅛-inch-wide saw cut is made on the face of the molding every 1 inch to a depth of ¼ inch

Items You Can Make

In addition to items you can purchase, there are several pieces you can make yourself by using some basic tools and accessories.

Wood half-rounds are often used to soften linear forms and create finials. For sizes up to 2 ½ inches, they are quite easy to fabricate using an electric drill with a hole saw accessory. For larger half rounds, I suggest using a jigsaw or scroll saw, if you have one. It's always best to start with a block of wood larger than the shape you need so you can clamp the work piece to a stable surface.

Moldings are somewhat delicate and require a finer grade of wood like select pine or poplar. Lower grades of pine with few imperfections will do in a pinch, but they may splinter when cut and crack when nailed. For cutting the designs, a small craft-type backsaw works great. If you have a bandsaw handy, this is the time to dust it off and cut several moldings in one go.

You will need an adequate means of support when cutting moldings by hand. A small bench-mounted vise could work, or you could make your molding from a piece that is longer than needed, and clamp it to a bench at the two unused ends. Always make sure your working conditions are safe, as even a hand tool can cause an injury.

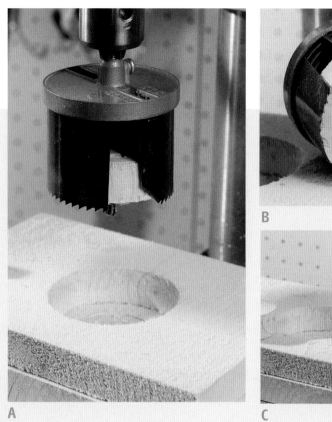

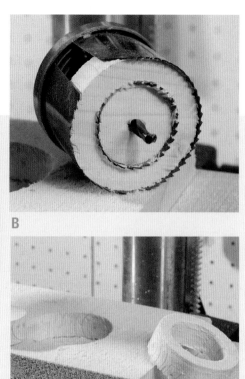

A

B

C

Predator Guards for Entry Holes

Predator guards are both functional and decorative. They can be made in almost any shape to add character and color to a design. You can create a simple predator guard, such as the one used in the Sticks and Blocks project on page 91, by drilling through the center of a square piece of pine with a 1½-inch spade drill bit.

Many of the projects in this book include a special combination hole that I call the **predator donut**. It consists of a circular ring with the center portion cut out to match a 1½-inch entry hole. The predator donut fits over the entry hole of the box, adding additional weather protection and security for the inhabitants inside. This special hole is easy to cut using two blades simultaneously in a hole saw.

The above photos demonstrate how you do it. Use a combination hole saw to drill through a piece of wood securely clamped onto a scrap piece (photo A). I'm using a drill press here, but a handheld drill works just as well. Photo B shows how the hole saw has cut through the wood. And, as you can see in photo C, removing the pieces gives you a round donut ready for sanding. You can also cut this donut in half to create a useful arch.

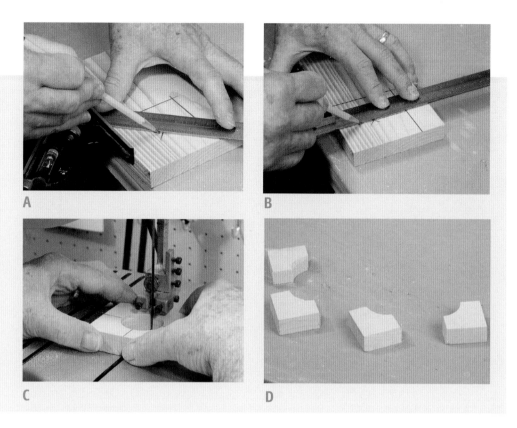

A

B

C

D

Brackets

Brackets are one of the features that can add a nice architectural touch to birdhouses. The first project in this book, Lattice and Brackets, requires (not surprisingly) that you make four brackets. The following is an easy method for making brackets that match exactly.

First, use a combination square to draw a 3-inch square at the corner of a piece of scrap pine board. Then, to find the center of the square, draw two short lines in the middle, going diagonally from opposite corners, as shown in photo A. Next, draw perpendicular lines through the center (as in photo B), first in one direction and then in the other.

With a 1½-inch spade bit, drill a hole through the middle of the center "X". Then cut through the perpendicular lines (as shown in photo C) to make the four brackets in photo D. I'm using a bandsaw to make the cuts, but you can use the saw of your choice.

Roofing Materials

One material you can use to create the look of a shingled roof is **cedar roof lattice**. You can fabricate such pieces from cedar stock. The photo at the top of page 42 shows how to rip cedar stock to the narrow width you'll need for roof pieces. You can also purchase pine lattice and paint or stain it, but it won't match the wonderful texture and range of colors of real cedar. If you're lucky, you can find an old house shutter with cedar slats to disassemble and cut to size.

Some projects have metal roofs. It's not true, as some believe, that metal roofs will roast nestlings. Actually, shiny metals reflect the rays of the sun, much as reflective glass does in high-rise office buildings. The two metals I prefer to use are 30-gauge **rolled copper sheet** and commercial **aluminum flashing**, also sold in rolls. Both are relatively inexpensive, especially flashing.

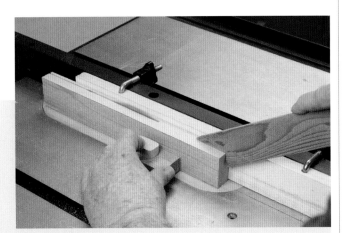

Ripping pieces of cedar lattice

They can be readily worked to fit any freeform shape, cut with household scissors, and secured with construction adhesive or small brass carpet tacks. You should wear gloves when working with this material, as the cut edges can be rough. To smooth rough edges, sanding with medium-grit paper will do the trick.

I mentioned earlier how the 6 x 6-inch copper-topped post cap is ideal for relatively narrow and tall square boxes. To fasten this cap, you simply squirt a bead of caulk or construction adhesive around the inner rim and push the post over your prepared box. That's all there is to it!

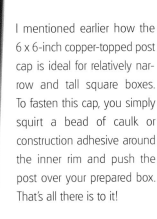

Aluminum flashing and rolled copper sheet

Finials

Once you put the roof on, you'll be using finials to crown the top of a number of the projects. Centuries ago in medieval Europe, buildings were constructed with finials on the top of a gable to ward off witches, who supposedly feared getting entangled on a finial and would go elsewhere. Nowadays, they are a final statement that says, "Hey, look at me, I'm something special!"

The finials illustrated here will later be referenced by their number to go in specific projects, but you can interchange them as you see fit. Even if the angle of the roof is different, you can alter the finial to suit a particular slope.

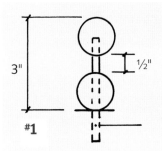

#1

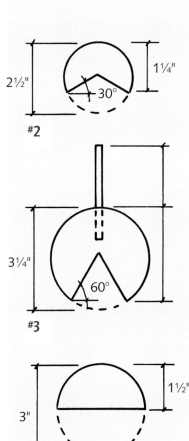

#2

#3

#4

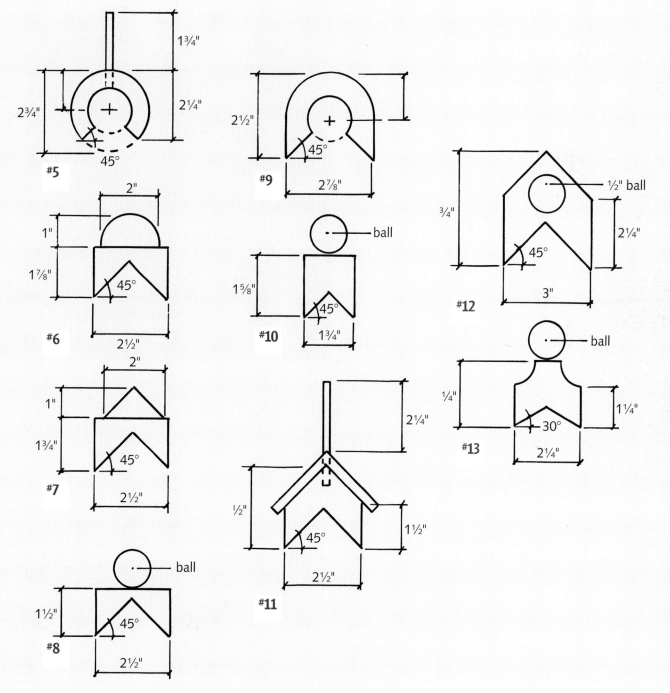

#5 — 1¾" / 2¾" / 2¼" / 45°

#9 — 2½" / 45° / 2⅞"

#12 — ½" ball / ¾" / 2¼" / 45° / 3"

#6 — 2" / 1" / 1⅞" / 45° / 2½"

#10 — ball / 1⅝" / 45° / 1¾"

#13 — ball / ¼" / 1¼" / 30° / 2¼"

#7 — 2" / 1" / 1¾" / 45° / 2½"

#11 — 2¼" / ½" / 45° / 1½" / 2½"

#8 — ball / 1½" / 45° / 2½"

Painting and Finishing Techniques

The birdhouses in this book get their unique looks from a combination of their architectural structures, added embellishments such as moldings and other pieces, and their colorful surface designs.

In the Projects section, I'll discuss some particular painting techniques such as stenciling (page 77) and decoupage (page 101). Here are some more general tips for painting and finishing:

▦ Remember, paint dries darker, so choose your color accordingly.

▦ Paint light areas first, followed by dark over light.

▦ Paint edges before flat areas.

▦ Paint in the direction of the wood grain unless a particular technique suggests otherwise.

▦ In general, smooth out your initial strokes as you paint, always starting off a wet edge.

▦ For masking areas, use painter's masking tape in lieu of the general household brand.

For durability, and a great selection of ready-mixed colors, you might want to try professional artist's acrylics made especially for fine art painting; these are not to be confused with craft-type acrylics. Most fine art and craft stores offer a wide selection to choose from. In addition, for an excellent sealer that gives a durable, waterproof, clear coat, I suggest you try clear acrylic medium. It brings out the luster in wood, especially the warm hues found in cedar.

Installing Your Birdhouse

Finally . . . the paint is dry! Now it's time to install your brand-new birdhouse.

You can support your nesting box on metal poles, wood posts, PVC tubes, or you can purchase a support. Poles are usually sold in sections varying from 18 to 24 inches per section and include a mounting flange. You can buy them in galvanized steel, aluminum, and coated steel, and in small diameters. Avoid small-diameter plastic poles, as they aren't very stable. For any pole, make sure the diameter doesn't look out of scale or too precarious when supporting a reasonably sized birdhouse.

When it comes to wood, several companies sell decorative posts for birdhouses that resemble country-style porch posts. You could buy a porch post, but that gets a bit expensive.

You can always make your own support. A four-inch-square pressure-treated wood post makes a very sturdy support, and they're easy to find and economical. You can also make your own metal post from galvanized steel or black iron pipe, topped off with an inverted floor flange. These items can be purchased from home improvement, plumbing, or hardware stores, and they're available in larger diameters more suitable to the scale of a nest box.

A 3-inch PVC tube is another possibility. Its slick surface automatically dissuades predators from climbing, so a predator guard is rarely needed. You can buy an inexpensive PVC floor drain flange that fits snugly inside the tube and serves as the underside mount for your birdhouse. One last mounting option is to find a fence post or dead tree for support.

Setting a Support

The simplest way to set any support is to dig a hole with a post digger or spade-point shovel. You'll need a hole 18 to 24 inches deep and about 4 inches wider than the support itself. After the hole is dug, place about 4 inches of gravel in the bottom for drainage. Set your post, and pour concrete all around it to fill the remaining space. In climates prone to frost, it's good practice to extend the post down an additional 6 inches below the frost line to prevent heaving.

If the soil in your area compacts well, you can set a wood post or PVC tube into the hole and tightly compact the removed soil around it for a snug fit. With a PVC tube it's a good idea to pour about 18 inches of stone or gravel into the tube to make the bottom more stable. Due to their small diameter, it's always advisable to set a metal post in concrete for stability.

However you set your support, make sure you use a level to get it straight. You don't want to spend the rest of your life looking out the window to check your nesting box with your head tilted to one side.

Baffles

When you attract birds, you become accountable for their security. By nature birds are cautious and recognize the dangers that might befall them. It's the danger they don't see that poses a problem. By properly placing a birdhouse, you can avoid the majority of threats from above from jumping predators. It's from below that you need to thwart those climbing critters.

The devices used to frustrate those predators are called baffles. They fall into three general categories, loosely described as saucers, cones, and tubes. For 4-inch square wood posts, a cone baffle (as shown in the photo below) is a very good choice or consider the 16-inch long cylinder type. Both are constructed of heavy metal so predators can't destroy them. For poles, polycarbonate plastic saucers are fine, but a better (if more expensive) choice is a metal pole cone or a 6-inch diameter steel tube. As mentioned earlier, PVC supports are difficult to grip for climbing and shouldn't need baffles. When placing your baffle, the top of it should be at least 4 feet above ground level and securely fastened to the support.

Mounting Your Birdhouse

I favor supporting a nesting box from below, for a simple reason. With the exception of Three for One house (page 98) and the Roosting Box (page 106), all the projects in this book are equipped with a removable base that provides easy access for cleaning and serves a dual purpose for mounting. The base can be attached to the top of a wood post with just one screw. Once the base is in place, you can set the nest box on it and easily attach it from underneath. If you use a flange-type support, you merely attach the flange to the underside of the removable base and then screw the base to the birdhouse. I use a couple of variations of the removable base, but the principle is always the same, and the concept of avoiding water intrusion should always be considered.

I don't recommend hanging birdhouses unless you want to attract wrens. Birds don't like movement when they're breeding and tend to avoid hanging boxes. The height to mount a nesting box is not a precise science. Look at the chart on page 25 for a range to choose from. I have mounted birdhouses anywhere from 5 to 15 feet above ground level, on wood posts and dead trees, and I have yet to find the magic distance.

The Choice Is Up to You

One last word here: in all the projects in this book, I want to encourage you to explore and experiment. Many of the parts and pieces discussed and illustrated can be interchanged from one project to another—including moldings, predator guards, and finials. You might also want to deviate from some of my color suggestions, and that's okay. If something doesn't quite work out the way I say it should, use your intuitive sense and devise your own unique solution. Now let's build some fantastic birdhouses!

The Projects

Lattice and Brackets

Cedar lattice and pine brackets distinguish this birdhouse from the other two in the cedar box series. The bracket is an old architectural feature re-emerging in today's building design, and it seemed a natural for this project. I started using lattice a few years ago when I found an old wooden window shutter. At the time, the thought struck me that the scale of the louvers would create an interesting roof texture for a birdhouse. Since it's difficult to find just louvers, I later decided to cut my own from 1-inch cedar stock, and I have never been disappointed with the results.

CUTTING LIST

Description	Quantity	Size	Cut From
Gable	2	¾ x 11 ¼ x 12	1 x 12 pine
Roof	2	½ x 12 x 12 ¼	1 x 12 trim board
Side	2	¾ x 6 x 6 ½	1 x 8 cedar
Base	1	¾ x 6 ½ x 6 ½	1 x 8 cedar
Front	2	¾ x 6 x 8	1 x 6 cedar
Blocks	4	1 x 1¼ x 1¼	scrap cedar
Brackets	4	¾ x 1½ x 1½	scrap pine
Trim	6	¾ x ½ x about 9	scrap cedar

Other Components

2 predator donuts: 2 ½-inch diameter with a 1½-inch opening (see page 40)

Finial #10 (see page 43)

Roof lattice, cut from cedar stock or ready-made (see page 41)

Instructions

1 Cut the basic cedar box pieces to the size indicated in figure 1 with the saw of your choice. After you've cut the fronts, drill the 1½-inch entry holes with the spade bit at the places indicated on the diagram.

2 Assemble the box using a bench hook or clamps to hold the pieces in position. Use the waterproof exterior glue and 1½-inch casing nails or trim-head screws. Make sure you fasten the sides to the fronts as shown in figure 1; otherwise, the gables won't fit properly.

3 Lay out the gable, as shown in figure 2, directly on the 1 x 12 pine board using the 45° drafting triangle, the carpenter's combination square, and a pencil. The angle determines the final dimensions, so follow the angle to achieve an accurate layout.

4 Before you cut out the gable, drill a hole at the center arch, at the point marked with a cross on figure 2. Use the hole saw with the 2 ½-inch blade. By making this cut first, you can use it as a large pilot hole for your jigsaw, which will allow you to cut out the rest of the archway and gable (as on figure 2).

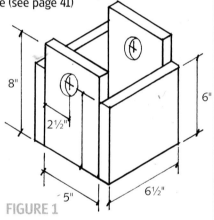

FIGURE 1

Materials

Waterproof exterior glue
Paint primer/sealer
Exterior latex paint, satin finish
Construction adhesive
Exterior wood filler
Acrylic medium

Tools & Accessories

Basic Tool Kit; Power Shop Tools
   (optional); and Safety Essentials
   (see page 18)
1½-inch spade bit
1½-inch trim screws
1½-inch casing nails
Hole saw with 1½- and
   2 ½-inch blades
¾-inch brads
1½-inch #8 zinc-coated
   Phillips-head screws (2)

TIP

After you've cut out the first gable, use it as a template to trace and lay out the second.

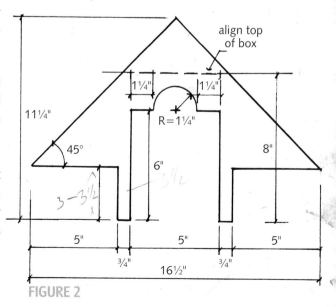

FIGURE 2

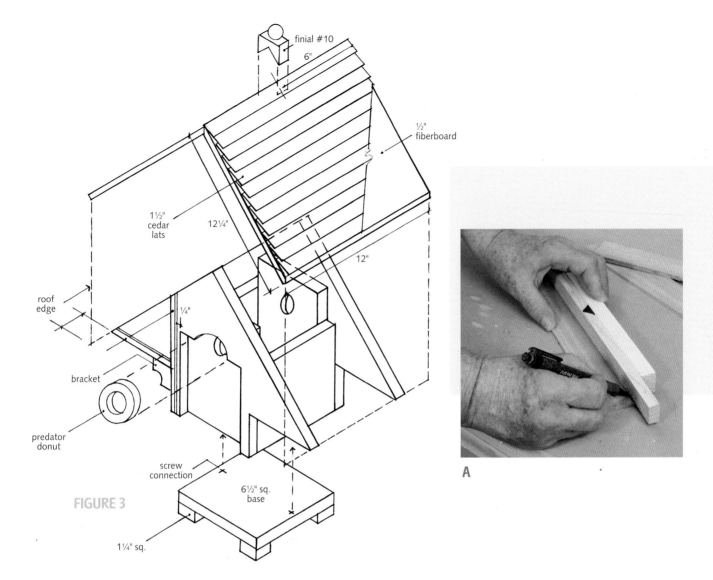

finial #10

6"

½" fiberboard

1½" cedar lats

12¼"

12"

roof edge

¼"

bracket

predator donut

screw connection

6½" sq. base

1¼" sq.

FIGURE 3

A

5 Prime both gables and then apply two coats of paint. It's easier to fill nail holes and touch them up later than it is to paint them after you've attached them to the cedar box.

6 Set the box and one of the gables together on a flat surface, aligned as in figure 3. Make sure the gable is centered over the entry hole. Add glue to the back of the gable and attach it to the cedar box with 1½-inch casing nails. Flip over the box and attach the other gable in the same way.

7 The roof consists of two parts: the support for the wood lattice and the wood lattice itself. To create the support roof, cut two pieces measuring 12¼ x 12 inches from the trim board. On one 12-inch end of each board, cut a 45° miter. This is so the two ends will meet in a miter joint at the peak.

8 Attach one roof piece at a time. Center the first piece on the gable/box assembly. Glue and nail the roof piece to the pine gable using 1½-inch casing nails. Align the second piece with the first, meeting at the peak, and attach it to the gable. You now have a solid base for attaching the wood lattice.

9 For this step, you'll need the cedar lattice you've made (as on page 41), or ready-made wood lattice you've stained with a semi-transparent cedar stain. Cut 20 strips at 12 inches long and about 1¾ inches wide. Attach 10 strips to each side of the roof, starting at the bottom edge, as follows:

▦ Mark a line at either end of each lattice piece, ½ inch from the top edge. In photo A, I use a jig I've made for this purpose, but any number of measuring tools can do the job.

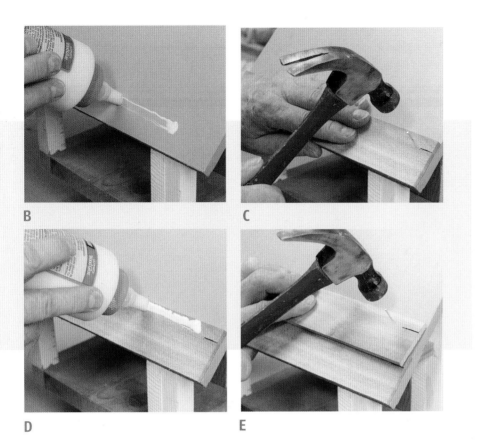

B

C

D

E

Spread a bead of glue along the roof where the first piece will go (photo B). Align the first lattice piece with the roof edge and hammer it on with four of the brads, starting about 1 inch from the edge (photo C).

Spread another bead of glue on the nailed-on piece above the two marks (photo D). Line up the next piece with its bottom edge on the marks, and nail it on with the brads (photo E).

When you get to the top of the roof, you will have to trim one or both of the final two pieces to a proper width to form a neatly fitting peak.

10 For an easy way to make the four brackets (shown in figure 3), see page 41. Attach two on each front with glue and finishing nails.

11 Make the two predator donuts (one for each front), as described on page 40. Attach one to each box front, as shown in figure 3, with glue and finishing nails.

12 For the front trim, cut a few lengths ½ inch wide by ¼ inch thick and at least 9 inches long from cedar scrap. Measure the strips to fit and cut the required angle cuts to line up with the bottom of the roof. A craft-type back saw and a small miter box works well for this. Attach the cedar trim strips to the gable with the glue and ¾-inch brads.

13 To complete the assembly, cut the base to the dimensions shown in figure 3. Cut four 1¼-inch square blocks and fasten them to the base with construction adhesive. By the inside corner of each block, drill a ¼-inch drain hole through the base block. Then drill two pilot holes in the base ⅜ inch from the edge on opposite sides (see figure 3). Screw the two 1½-inch #8 zinc-coated Phillips-head screws through the pilot holes to attach the base to the box. You'll be able to remove the screws easily for routine maintenance.

14 At the center point of the roof, attach finial #10 (see page 43) with construction adhesive. Countersink all visible nails and/or screws. Fill the holes with wood filler and sand smooth. Touch up any marred paint. Brush on two coats of acrylic medium over all the cedar parts to seal the wood and accentuate the rich quality of the natural cedar.

Marbles and Chips

Y ou can enhance a basic cedar box in a variety of ways. In this project, although the main design element is the gable, the roof takes on a personality of its own, adding something unique to the total assembly. With a pattern of ready-made floral marbles and stained glass chips, a humble roof can become a work of art. You'll find a template for this decorative roof pattern that you can enlarge for use on page 124, or just create your own pattern to suit your taste.

CUTTING LIST

Description	Quantity	Size	Cut From
Gable	2	¾ x 10 ½ x 14	1 x 12 pine
Roof	2	½ x 10 ½ x 12	½ x 12 trim board
Side	2	¾ x 6 x 6 ½	1 x 8 cedar
Front	2	¾ x 5 x 8	1 x 6 cedar
Base	1	¾ x 6 ½ x 6 ½	1 x 8 cedar
Blocks	4	1 x 1¼ x 1¼	scrap cedar

Other Components

2 predator guards: ¾-inch segments cut from 3 ½-inch diameter PVC tube

Finial #9 (see page 43)

Instructions

1 Using the saw of your choice, cut the basic cedar box components to the dimensions indicated on the cutting list and figure 1. After you've cut the fronts, drill the 1½-inch entry holes with the spade bit.

2 Assemble the box as arranged in figure 1, using a bench hook or clamps to hold the pieces in position. Use the waterproof exterior glue and 1½-inch casing nails or trim screws.

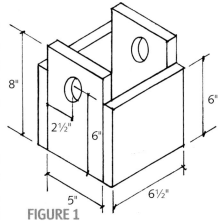

FIGURE 1

3 Lay out the gables directly on the 1 x 12 pine board with the dimensions shown in figure 2, using the 45° drafting triangle and the carpenter's combination square. Be sure to follow the angle correctly to achieve an accurate layout and the proper dimensions.

4 Before you cut out each gable, drill a hole at the center arch, at the point marked with a cross on figure 2. Use a hole saw with the 2 ½-inch blade. By making this cut first, you can use it as a large pilot hole for your jigsaw, which will allow you to cut out the rest of the archway and gable. You can use the first gable as a template for cutting the second.

Materials

Waterproof exterior glue

1½-inch casing nails or trim-head screws

Paint primer/sealer

Exterior acrylic latex paint, satin finish

1-inch PVC angle trim, 12 inches long

Construction adhesive

¼-inch square wood stock

½-inch brads

3 ½-inch diameter PVC tube, ¾ inch long

Exterior wood filler

Acrylic medium

Mosaic pattern template (optional)

Floral marbles and mosaic glass tesserae (available at craft stores; the project shown uses ¾-inch marbles and ¾- and ⅜-inch tesserae)

Tools and Accessories

Basic Tool Kit; Power Shop Tools (optional); and Safety Essentials (see page 18)

1½-inch spade bit

Hole saw, 2 ½-inch diameter blade

1½-inch #8 zinc-coated Phillips-head screws (2)

Craft knife with #11 blade

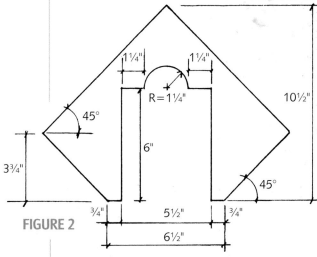

FIGURE 2

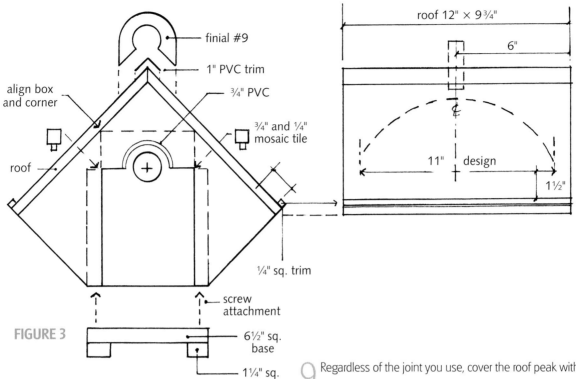

finial #9

1" PVC trim

¾" PVC

align box
and corner

¾" and ¼"
mosaic tile

roof

⅟4" sq. trim

screw
attachment

FIGURE 3

6½" sq.
base

1¼" sq.

roof 12" × 9¾"

6"

11"   design

1½"

5 Prime both gables and then apply two coats of paint. After the gables are attached, fill in any nail holes and touch up the paint.

6 Fasten the gables to the cedar box with the casing nails and glue, with the bottom of the gable aligned to the bottom of the box. It is critical, though, to make sure no part of the top of the cedar box protrudes above the gable. If any part does, the roof won't fit properly.

7 Now cut the roof pieces. From the trim board, cut two 9 ¾-inch by 12-inch pieces, with one 12-inch end of each piece cut to a 45° miter, as can be seen in figure 3. If you prefer the easier butt joint, make the pieces without a miter, but cut one piece at 10 inches instead of 10 ½ inches.

8 Attach the roof one piece at a time. Center one of the roof pieces over the box/gable assembly. Fasten it to the gable with glue and 1½-inch nails. Align the second roof section to exactly meet the first, and then glue and nail it in place.

9 Regardless of the joint you use, cover the roof peak with a 1-inch x 12-inch piece of PVC angle trim. Trim board joints are always suspect. Glue the trim over the joint with construction adhesive. Tape the trim down while the glue sets for an even, secure fit.

10 At the very edge of the roof on either side, attach a 12-inch strip of ¼-inch square wood stock, preferably poplar. Glue and nail each piece with ½-inch brads.

11 Over the gable archway, just above each entry hole, use construction adhesive to attach the ¾-inch segment of the PVC tube, cut in half, as a predator guard.

12 Cut the access base to the size shown in figure 3. Cut four 1¼-inch-square base blocks and attach them to the bottom of the base with 1½-inch casing nails or construction adhesive. By the inside corner of each block, drill a ¼-inch drain hole through the base block.

13 Drill a pilot hole at two opposite edges of the base, each ⅜ inch from the edge. Screw the two 1½-inch #8 zinc-coated Phillips-head screws through the pilot holes to attach the base to the box. You'll be able to remove the screws easily for routine maintenance.

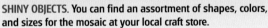

SHINY OBJECTS. You can find an assortment of shapes, colors, and sizes for the mosaic at your local craft store.

14 Countersink the exposed nail or screw heads. Fill the holes with exterior wood filler and sand smooth before you begin painting. Coat all the exposed cedar pieces with two coats of acrylic medium.

15 Now paint the roof with one coat of primer and two coats of acrylic latex. When it's dry, you can lay out the mosaic pattern on the roof surface.

16 Enlarge the mosaic design pattern provided on page 124 to the size indicated or design one of your own. Whatever pattern you choose, you can use it as a template for the mosaics by cutting out the shapes with a craft knife. Lay the stencil on the roof and, with a soft pencil, outline the shapes. Using the birdhouse photo above for reference, set the floral marbles and glass chips in the pattern. Glue each piece with construction adhesive, pressing down firmly to set each piece in place. Be careful not to squeeze excess glue on the roof, as it's sloppy and difficult to clean.

TIP

Don't move the birdhouse for at least 30 minutes after gluing, to give the adhesive a chance to work. Glue only one side of the roof at a time. After 24 hours, the adhesive should be rock-hard.

17 As a final touch, cut finial #9 (see page 43) and attach it to the roof at the center point with 1-inch nails or construction adhesive. Paint the finial, and the trim, in the color shown or one of your choice.

Board and Batten Shingle House

This birdhouse derives its name from the roof design and the material used: crude cedar shingles normally used as leveling shims. I like it for its off-beat character and rustic appeal, but its real attraction is the dual-function roosting shelf that provides protection for small birds during inclement weather and also serves as a permanent base for the nesting box. This project is the third in a series that starts with a basic cedar box. The design requires accurate measurements and some patience, but the results are rewarding.

CUTTING LIST

Description	Quantity	Size	Cut From
Gable	2	¾ x 7 ½ x 15	1 x 10 pine
Roof (base)	2	½ x 11 ¼ x 12	½ x 12 trim board
Roosting shelf	1	¾ x 7 ¾ x 15 ½	1 x 10 cedar
Side	2	1 x 6 x 6 ½	1 x 8 cedar
Base	1	¾ x 6 ½ x 6 ½	1 x 8 cedar
Front	2	¾ x 5 x 8	1 x 6 cedar
Blocks	4	1 x 1¼ x 1¼	scrap cedar

Other Components

2 predator guards: ¾-inch segments cut from 3 ½-inch diameter PVC tube

Finial #9 (see page 43)

Cedar roof shingles (shims), sold by the bundle, cut as instructed

Instructions

1 Cut the basic cedar box pieces to the size indicated in figure 1, with the saw of your choice. After you've cut the fronts, drill the 1½-inch entry holes with a spade bit.

2 Assemble the box using a bench hook or clamps to hold the pieces in position. Use the waterproof exterior glue and 1½-inch casing nails or trim-head screws. Make sure you fasten the sides to the fronts as shown in figure 1; otherwise, the gables won't fit properly.

3 Lay out the gable directly on the 1 x 12 pine board, as shown in figure 2, using the 45° drafting triangle and the carpenter's combination square. The angle determines the dimensions, so follow the angle to achieve an accurate layout.

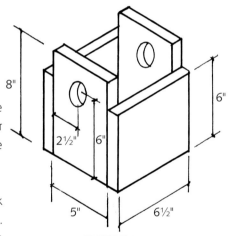

8"

6"

2½" 6"

5" 6½"

FIGURE 1

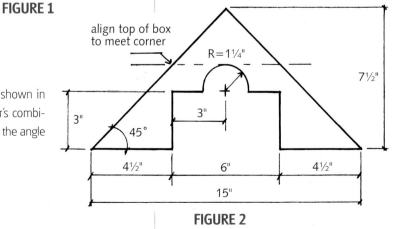

align top of box to meet corner

R = 1¼"

7½"

3"

45°

3"

4½" 6" 4½"

15"

FIGURE 2

Materials

Waterproof exterior glue
Paint primer/sealer
Exterior acrylic latex paint, satin finish
Construction adhesive
½-inch diameter wood dowel, 4 feet long
3 ½-inch diameter PVC tube
¼-inch square wood stock
Exterior wood filler
Acrylic medium

Tools and Accessories

Basic Tool Kit; Power Shop Tools (optional); and Safety Essentials (see page 18)
1 ½-inch spade bit
1 ½-inch casing nails or trim-head screws
Hole saw with 2 ½-inch blade
½-inch brad-point bit
½-, ⅝-, and 1-inch brads
1 ½-inch #8 zinc-coated Phillips-head screws (2)

4 Before you cut out the gable, drill a hole at the center arch, at the point marked with a cross on figure 2. Use the hole saw with the 2½-inch blade. By making this cut first, you can use it as a large pilot hole for your jigsaw, which will allow you to cut out the rest of the archway and gable.

5 Prime both gables and then apply two coats of paint. It's easier to fill nail holes and touch them up later than it is to paint them after you've attached them to the cedar box.

6 Measure three inches up from the bottom of the cedar box. This is the line where you'll attach the gable. Make sure that the top of the box doesn't protrude beyond the slope of the gable. If it does, the roof won't fit properly. Add glue to the back of each gable and attach them to the cedar box with 1½-inch casing nails, as shown in figure 3.

7 Cut the piece for the roosting shelf. If you have a table saw, now is the time to use it. If you don't have one, use a saw with a properly clamped guide. It's important that this piece has square corners and accurate dimensions.

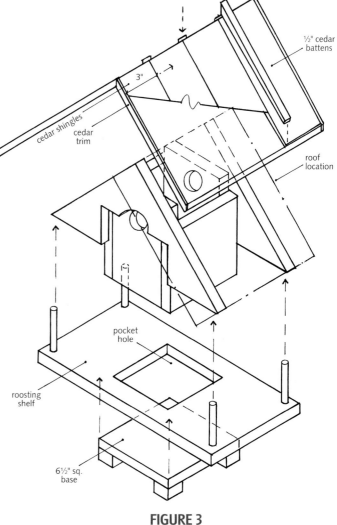

FIGURE 3

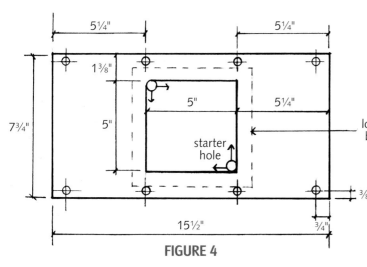

FIGURE 4

8 Clamp the roosting shelf piece to a sturdy bench and carefully measure where to drill and cut. Refer to figure 4 for the measurements. To begin the center cut, drill two starter holes with a ½-inch brad point bit at opposite corners of the square. Then cut out the 5 x 5-inch square with the jigsaw. Place a scrap piece of wood under the roosting shelf and drill the ½-inch dowel holes all the way through.

9 To attach the gable/box assembly to the roosting shelf, spread glue on the underside of the cedar box and place it directly over the 5-inch square hole. From underneath the roosting shelf, screw the pieces together with 1½-inch trim-head screws.

10 Take approximate measurements for the dowels, from where they will meet the bottom of the gable down through the thickness of the shelf. Cut each dowel piece about ½ inch longer than this measurement. Pre-paint the dowel lengths. When they're dry, push them one at a time up through the drilled holes. When one is halfway up, add a bead of glue to its top. Then push it firmly up against the underside of the gable, making sure it's straight. Drive a 1-inch brad through the edge of the roosting shelf to secure the dowel. Repeat this step for each dowel. When you're done, turn the assembly on its side and remove any excess lengths with a craft-type backsaw so that the bottom of the shelf is flush.

11 Now make the roof. The roof consists of the support for the shingles and the shingles themselves. To create the support roof, cut two pieces measuring 11 ¼ x 12 inches from the 12-inch wide trim board. On each 11 ¼-inch end, cut a 45° miter for joining the boards at the top of the gable. Attach one board at a time to the pine gable, using the glue and 1½-inch casing nails.

12 From the bundle of rough shingles, find some with a similar profile—approximately the same tapered thickness from top to bottom. Select enough to cover the entire roof. Cut the shingles into eight 3 x 11 ½-inch sections. Cut the thicker tapered end of each shingle at a 45° angle for a snug fit at the peak.

13 Glue and nail (using the ⅝-inch brads) each shingle section, side by side, across the 12-inch width of the roof on both sides.

14 From your shingle bundle, select one decent piece and cut it into six ½-inch wide strips, each measuring 12 inches long. Miter the thinner end at a 45° angle where it will meet the gable peak. Glue and nail the strips over the seams of the shingles to create a board-and-batten effect. If done correctly, the battens should be thinner at the peak and thicker at the bottom of the roof. To cover the facing edge of the gable, cut four shingle strips ½-inch wide by ¼-inch thick. Fasten them to the gable with ½-inch brads. Complete the roof by attaching the finial #9 over the center batten strip with construction adhesive.

MIX THINGS UP. This birdhouse combines the roosting shelf and columns of the Board and Batten with the shingle-style roof of the Lattice and Brackets (page 48), all topped off by a finial different from either.

15 To complete the assembly, cut the base to the dimensions shown in figure 3. Cut four 1¼-inch square blocks and fasten them to the base with construction adhesive. By the inside corner of each block, drill a ¼-inch drain hole through the base block. Then drill two pilot holes in the base ⅜ inch from the edge on opposite sides. Screw the two 1½-inch #8 zinc-coated Phillips-head screws through the pilot holes to attach the base to the shelf. You'll be able to remove the screws easily for routine maintenance.

16 To make the predator guards, cut the ¾-inch PVC pipe in half and attach each segment to the gable directly over the entry hole with construction adhesive. Complete the trim with ¼-inch square wood stock, starting from the outside of the predator guard, going around the perimeter of the archway, and along the bottom of the gable to the roof, forming a continuous trim line. (See the photo on page 56.) Glue and nail the trim with ½-inch brads to the gable.

17 Countersink all your visible nails or screws. Fill the holes with exterior wood filler and sand smooth. Touch up any marred paint. Brush on two coats of acrylic medium over all visible cedar parts; this will seal the wood and bring out its luster.

Recycled Triangles

S ome people might associate this project with a church, and I can see why, as the triangular form has a long and storied history in church architecture. However, in designing this project, I was intrigued with recycling the leftover pieces cut from the gables. I wanted a design that would take the Basic Box to another level and yet stay simple enough to build easily. This project appears more complex than it really is.

CUTTING LIST

Description	Quantity	Size	Cut From
Front	2	¾ x 7 ¼ x 14 ¼	1 x 8 pine
Side	2	¾ x 5 ¾ x 6	1 x 8 pine
Roof	2	¾ x 7 ¼ x about 14 ½	1 x 8 pine
Base	1	¾ x 5 ¾ x 7	1 x 8 pine
Trim	1	¼ x ¼ x 48	poplar stock

Other Components

4 recycled gable parts

2 handmade half-rounds, 4 inches each (E in figure 2)

Handmade or store-bought M3 molding, 12 inches long (G)

Half-round molding, 8 inches long (A)

4 pieces of screen molding, 4 ½ inches long (D)

Cove molding, 5 feet long (B)

4 pieces of #1 chair rail (see page 38) (H)

4 pieces of #4 chair rail (see page 38) (F)

Finial #3 (see page 42)

Materials

Waterproof exterior glue

Construction adhesive

Acrylic latex caulk

1 ¼ -inch wood balls (4)

Exterior wood filler

Medium-grade sandpaper

Paint primer/sealer

Exterior acrylic latex paint, satin finish

Tools and Accessories

Basic Tool Kit; Power Shop Tools
   (optional); and Safety Essentials
   (see page 18)

1 ½-inch spade bit

½-inch brad-point bit

1 ½-inch casing nails

1 ½- and 1 ¾-inch trim-head screws (4)

1 ½-inch #8 zinc-coated Phillips-head
   screws (2)

½- and ¾-inch brads

Drawing compass

Instructions

1 Review figure 1, and you'll see that this birdhouse starts out as a Basic Box with 60° integral gables (Variation 2). Using one 8-foot-long 1 x 8 board, you can lay out all the required pieces using the carpenter's combination square, 60° drafting triangle, and metal ruler. Allow enough space between each piece for your saw cut. And re-member that you will need to save the cut-off gable corners to use later in the project.

2 If you have a table saw, use it to cut the gable fronts, sides, and base. It'll help you achieve clean, straight edges, especially on the recycled gable pieces. If you don't have a table saw, use a handsaw or a jigsaw, but cut carefully.

3 Using the 1½-inch spade bit, drill the entry holes on both fronts as indicated in figure 1. Using the ½-inch brad-point bit, drill two ½-inch air holes in each of the two sides, at the locations shown in figure 1.

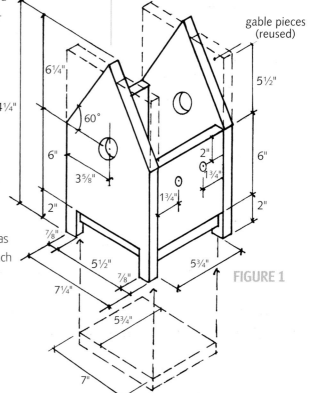

gable pieces
(reused)

FIGURE 1

4 Assemble the Basic Box, one front and one side at a time. Refer to figure 1 to position the pieces properly. (For example, the bottom of the sides will be 2 inches above the bottom of the fronts.) Glue a side and front together and fasten the joint with 1½-inch casing nails. Repeat for the other front and side, and then join the two halves with glue and 1½-inch casing nails. Use a bench hook or adjustable clamps for support.

5 To attach the recycled triangles, first cut ¾ inch off the bottom of each, making the length 5 ½ inches. Spread a bead of construction adhesive on the long length of triangle and position it ¾ inch back from the front, aligned with the slope of the gable (refer to figure 2). Secure the triangle to the side with a 1½-inch trim-head screw located 1½ inches from the top of the triangle. Repeat this step for each recycled piece.

6 To find the exact length for each side of the roof, measure the box along the slope from the peak of the gable to the bottom of one of the recycled triangles. Cut one end of each side to make a 60° miter joint. (See the diagrams in figure 3 for the steps for cutting this joint.) After you cut the joint, attach the first roof section by applying glue to the gable slopes and nailing the roof to them with 1½-inch casing nails. Before you attach the second section, run a bead of caulk along the edge of the first roof section and firmly butt the second piece to it. Then glue and nail the second section.

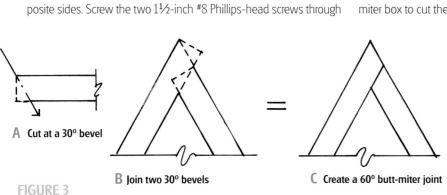

finial #3

roof 7¼" × 14½"

A

B

C

C

D

E

F

D

G

H

gable pieces

D

FIGURE 2

7 Cut lengthwise down the peak to create a flat surface ¾ to 1 inch wide; a jigsaw works best for this. Seal this joint with a thin layer of caulk. The roof should be flush with the front face of each gable.

8 Position the base beneath the box to correspond with the sides. Drill two pilot holes in the base ¼ inch from the edge on opposite sides. Screw the two 1½-inch #8 Phillips-head screws through

the pilot holes to attach the base to the box; this will allow you to remove the screws later for routine maintenance.

9 Now it's time to embellish the box. Working from the roof down, lay out finial #3 (see page 42). Glue it to the peak in the center of the roof with construction adhesive. Use the backsaw and small miter box to cut the molding and chair rail pieces. Cut the half-round molding to size. Attach them with glue and ¾-inch brads, per figure 2 and the main photo. Cut the cove molding to size for each gable end, and then miter the pieces for the peak. Glue and nail in place. Cut a piece of ¼-inch square stock and glue it at the bottom edge of each roof section. Cut and glue another piece down the center of the roof on both sides. Nail the pieces with ½-inch brads.

A **Cut at a 30° bevel**

B **Join two 30° bevels**

=

C **Create a 60° butt-miter joint**

FIGURE 3

62

10 Cut the numbered chair rail pieces according to the sizes indicated on page 38. Working on the fronts, from the bottom up, first attach chair rail piece #1 with construction adhesive. Add the screen molding. Directly above, add chair rail piece #4. Attach them with glue and ¾-inch brads. To finish the front embellishments, add the 4-inch half-round, laid out with a compass and cut with a jigsaw. Remember to clamp the scrap piece to a solid surface before you cut the half-rounds. Glue and nail the half-rounds in place with 1½-inch casing nails. Custom cut the screen molding for the recycled triangles, and then glue and nail them in place with ¾-inch brads. If you're making the M3 molding, refer to page 39. Attach the M3 molding to each front edge of the base with glue and ¾-inch brads.

11 Drill a pilot hole in each of the four 1¼-inch wood balls. Attach them to the legs using glue and 1¾-inch casing nails.

12 Countersink all exposed nails. Fill the holes with exterior wood filler and sand smooth. Prime all exposed surfaces with one coat of paint primer. Let dry. Follow with two coats of exterior acrylic latex paint in the colors shown or those of your own choice.

Birds and Food

When it comes to food for birds, natural sources are best. If you want to attract birds to your garden or yard, learn what plants, bushes, and trees are sources of natural food like berries, fruits, and seeds. Try to grow flowers that will attract the insects that form a main part of a cavity-nesting bird's diet. Include a seasonal supply of food as well as year-round sources.

During the winter months, bird feeders are a good substitute for natural sources. The food you provide depends on the bird you're trying to attract. Most wild birds prefer oil-rich sunflower seeds, and they're also fond of suet, fruits, jelly mealworms, and baked goods. By the way, it's a myth that birds will swell up and die from eating rice thrown at weddings. It's also not true that birds will become dependent on your feeders and will starve without the food you provide. Birds are independent creatures and will continue to seek out natural sources. After all, what do you think they do when you absentmindedly forget to restock your feeder?

The Temple

Years ago, while undertaking architectural research on the Yucatan Peninsula, I had the good fortune to visit several ancient Mayan sites. I was particularly fascinated with the temple structures—square in form, deeply set doorways, and surfaces adorned with richly carved ornamentation. It's strange how memories linger; in some respects, I link this design to my Mayan experience. It's simple in form, contains setback doorways—entry holes for birds actually—and is enriched with surface embellishments.

CUTTING LIST

Description	Quantity	Size	Cut From
Platform	1	¾ x 10½ x 10½	1 x 12 pine
Front	2	¾ x 8 x 8⅜	1 x 10 pine
Base	1	¾ x 9¼ x 9¼	1 x 10 pine
Side	2	¾ x 6¼ x 8⅜	1 x 10 pine
Roof	2	¾ x 7 x 11¼	1 x 8 pine
Setback doorway	2	¾ x 4 x 6¾	1 x 6 pine
Gable	2	¾ x 3 x 10½	1 x 4 pine
Trim	5	¼ x ¼ x 10½	stock poplar
Blocks	4	¾ x 1¼ x 1¼	scrap pine

Other Components

#5 chair rail pieces (see page 38)

#7 chair rail pieces (see page 38)

M4 molding (see page 39)

¼-inch square trim, purchased or made

Finial #11 (see page 43)

Materials

Waterproof exterior glue

3-inch standard chair rail molding

Shoe molding

1¼-inch diameter wood half-ball (2)

Construction adhesive

Exterior wood filler

Paint primer/sealer

Exterior acrylic latex paint, satin finish

Tools and Accessories

Basic Tool Kit; Power Shop Tools
(optional); and Safety Essentials
(see page 18)

Hole saw with 2½-inch blade

1½-inch spade bit

½-inch brad-point bit

½-, ¾-, and 1-inch brads

1½-inch casing nails

1½-inch #8 zinc-coated Phillips-head
screws (2)

Drawing compass

Instructions

1 Lay out the Basic Box pieces as indicated in figure 1: fronts, sides, roof sections, platform, gables, and the setback doorway pieces. Lay out the chamfered base as shown in figure 3. You will need to cut the fronts and sides to exactly the same height. Use the carpenter's combination square, 30° triangle, and metal ruler to help.

2 Cut the straight-edged pieces with the saw of your choice. You can cut the gables, roof miters, and the chamfered base with a jigsaw if you're careful, although a table saw works better. To make the archway, use the hole saw with a 2½-inch blade to cut out the circular portion, and then use the jigsaw to complete it. Clamp the setback doorway sections to a bench with a scrap piece of wood underneath and drill an entry hole in each with the 1½-inch spade bit. Then drill the air holes in the side pieces as indicated in figure 1 with the ½-inch brad-point bit.

3 Before you assemble the box, fasten the setback doorways to the inside surface of each front with glue and 1-inch brads. Glue and nail—with 1½-inch casing nails—the fronts to the sides using a clamp or bench hook for support.

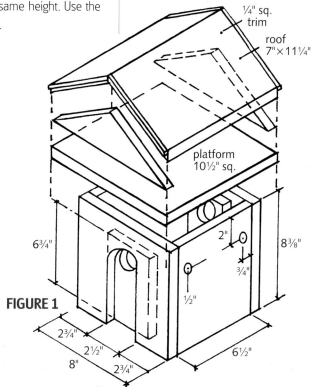

FIGURE 1

4 Spread a bead of glue on the long edge of each gable and nail the gables to the platform by using 1 ½-inch casing nails at the shallow end of the slope first, then from the underside for a solid connection. Attach the platform on top of the box by placing glue on the top edge of the front and side pieces. With the steel ruler, set the platform so that it overhangs 1¼ inches on all four sides. On the top of platform, mark a line 1⅝ inches from the outside edge. Drive 1½-inch casing nails through the platform into the box. Now attach the 1¼-inch wood blocks to the bottom of the chamfered base with construction adhesive.

5 Add the roof sections, one at a time. Spread a bead of glue on one slope of both gables (on the same side, of course). Fasten the first roof section to the gables, allowing a ⅜-inch overhang on the front of each gable. Nail in place with 1½-inch casing nails. Repeat for the second roof section.

6 Turn the box upside down and center the base on the box so the sides and front align evenly. Drill two pilot holes through the base about ⅞ inch from the edge on opposite sides to secure the base to the sides. Insert the two 1½-inch #8 zinc-coated Phillips-head screws in the pilot holes until they engage the sides. If the fit is right, detach the base; you'll add it back on later.

7 Now for the embellishments and trim. Using a compass, draw a 3 ½-inch-diameter half-round on a scrap block of wood. Clamp the block down and cut the circle halfway around with a jigsaw. Use a hole saw with the 2 ½-inch blade to cut out the center, leaving a ½-inch-thick half circle. With the jigsaw, cut the half circle away from the block. Repeat to make another half-round. Glue and nail each piece (D in figure 3)—using 1½-inch casing nails—directly over each entry hole to match with the archway.

8 Using a craft-type backsaw and small miter box, cut four #7 (E in the diagram) pieces of chair rail molding to size, as shown on page 38. Cut two 10 ½-inch pieces of chair rail #5 (B in the diagram) with a table saw or jigsaw.

FIGURE 2

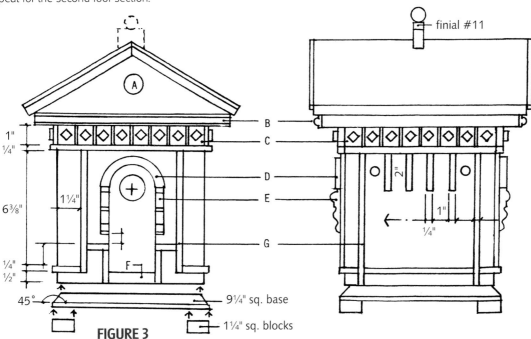

FIGURE 3

9 Attach a ½-inch-wide section of #5 chair rail molding to each front edge of the platform, as indicated in figure 3 (B in the diagram), using glue and 1-inch brads.

10 Fabricate the M4 molding (C in the diagram) as explained on page 39, using ¼-inch poplar. Make four identical molding strips, which should create a complete band around the box. Glue and nail each molding strip in place with 1-inch brads. Drive the nails in the slot space to avoid splitting the small squares.

11 Add all the ¼-inch square trim (G in the diagram). Start from the upper portion of the box, immediately below the M4 molding. Custom cut the pieces for a proper fit and carefully follow the birdhouse's dimensions and the arrangement shown in figure 3. You will need patience and time, but you will be pleased with the results. Fasten the pieces with glue and ½-inch brads.

12 Cut two 2 ⅝-inch pieces of shoe molding for the threshold at the bottom of each setback doorway. Glue and nail in place with a 1-inch brad. Also glue and nail the 1¼-inch wood half-balls in the center of each gable. Finish the embellishments with finial #11 (see page 43). Glue it with construction adhesive to the center point of the roof.

13 Countersink all exposed nails and screws. Fill the holes with exterior wood filler and sand smooth. Apply one coat of paint primer to all exposed surfaces. Let dry. Apply two coats of exterior acrylic latex paint, using the colors shown or colors of your preference.

Birds and Water

Birds obtain water from their food, dew on vegetation and the ground, or from natural sources like ponds and streams. To provide water, birdbaths are fine, but dripping or moving water is even better for attracting birds and providing for their needs. You can create a small water garden by sinking a pool liner in the ground and adding a pump with a water-spraying nozzle. For winter use, you might add a small immersible heater to your birdbath or pool. Whatever you decide, here are a few tips to consider when providing water:

- Place your water source in an open area, but make sure shrubs and bushes are nearby, within 10 feet, for escape.

- Elevate your birdbath to allow birds to watch out for predators.

- Change the water in a birdbath at least once a week.

- Clean your birdbath with soap or chlorine bleach, but make sure you rinse it thoroughly before refilling.

- The maximum depth of water useful for birds is 2 to 3 inches.

- For smooth birdbaths, like those made of metal or pool liners, provide gravel and rocks for grip and footing.

- Never use chemicals to control algae or prevent freezing.

- Position your birdbath in a shady location to minimize evaporation and the growth of algae.

Acorn

This pleasant shape now reminds me of an acorn, but the design didn't start out that way. It's based on the three-sided box—two sides and a removable base. The roof is made from 30-gauge copper sheet, which is very pliable; you can easily cut it with a pair of household scissors. But the copper is subject to dents and creases, so you must handle it gently. To offset this problem, I added wood half-rounds over the copper. These add strength and texture, even if they make the design look like an acorn.

CUTTING LIST

Description	Quantity	Size	Cut From
Front	2	¾ x 8 ½ x 12 ¾	1 x 10 pine
Side	2	¾ x 5 x 5 ¾	1 x 6 pine
Base	1	¾ x 5 x 6 ¼	1 x 6 pine
Applied arch	2	¾ x 4 ¾ x 7 ½	1 x 6 pine

Other Components

2 predator donuts: 2 ½-inch diameter with a 1 ½-inch opening (see page 40)

Instructions

1 Use a copy machine to enlarge the acorn shape in figure 2 to the size indicated onto heavyweight paper or cardstock. Cut out the shape with the scissors or craft knife.

2 Use the shape as a stencil on a 1 x 10 board that's at least 30 inches long. With a soft pencil, trace the shape twice on the board (see photo A); you'll use one piece for the back and one for the front. Before making your cuts, mark all the crosshairs shown in figure 2 on each piece with a nail hole. These spots locate the pilot holes for attaching the sides and drilling the entry hole. Cut out the acorn shapes with a jigsaw or scroll saw (see photo B).

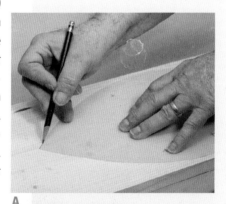

A

B

3 On a 1 x 6 board that's three feet long, lay out the sides, base, and two arch pieces (see figures 1 and 2). Use the metal ruler with the carpenter's combination square for the base and sides. To create a template for the arch, cut out the top portion of the paper acorn shape and use it to trace two arches.

Materials

Construction adhesive
Waterproof exterior glue
Cove molding
30-gauge copper sheet,
    8 ½ x 14 ¾ inches
Half-round molding, 10 feet
Exterior wood filler
Medium grade sandpaper
Paint primer/sealer
Exterior acrylic latex paint, satin finish

Tools and Accessories

Basic Tool Kit; Power Shop Tools
    (optional); and Safety Essentials
    (see page 18)
Craft knife
Household scissors
Soft pencil
1 ½-inch spade bit
⅛-inch brad point bit
1 ½ -inch #8 zinc-coated Phillips-head
    screws (2)
1 ½ -inch trim-head screws
⅝-inch brass linoleum nails
Hole saw with 2 ½- and 1 ½ -inch
blades
1-inch brads

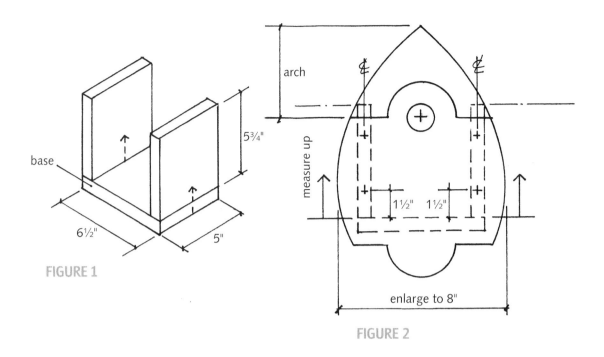

base

6½"

5"

5¾"

FIGURE 1

arch

measure up

1½"   1½"

enlarge to 8"

FIGURE 2

4 Cut out the arches with a jigsaw or scroll saw. With the straight-edged sections, you can use a handsaw instead.

5 Drill the entry hole at the marked location for both acorn shapes using a 1½-inch spade bit. With the ⅛-inch brad-point bit, drill holes all the way through the remaining crosshair marks on each arch. Turn the pieces over. Mark a point 1½ inches down from each bottom hole and draw a horizontal line connecting the marks. This establishes the baseline for setting your sides. For the vertical alignment, draw a line connecting the pilot holes. This establishes the centerline for the sides.

6 Temporarily assemble the three-sided box by drilling pilot holes in the base for the two 1½-inch #8 Phillips-head screws. Set the base flush with the sides and attach the three pieces together (see figure 1 for the arrangement). Spread construction adhesive on just the vertical edges of the two sides and attach the first front, using the guide lines. Using both hands, carefully turn it over. The construction adhesive will keep the box from slipping. From the front side, screw in two 1½-inch trim-head screws into the pilot holes to fasten the box to the front. Turn the box over and repeat to attach the second front. Loosen the base to make sure you can still remove it easily for maintenance.

7 Attach the arches where indicated (see figure 2) with glue and 1½-inch trim-head screws. Use a craft-type backsaw and small miter box to custom cut pieces of cove molding to fit under the bottom of each arch. Fasten the molding with glue and 1-inch brads.

8 Cut two 2½-inch predator donuts with the hole saw (see page 40 for details). Attach one to each side with construction adhesive.

TIP

You may want to wait to add the predator donuts until after you paint the main box. If so, paint the donuts separately (see project photo).

9 Fold the copper sheet in half. At the mid-point, use your hands to make a ¾-inch standing seam using a ¾-inch block of wood as your guide for the reverse fold. This material creases easily, so you shouldn't have much trouble making the standing seam. You can always pound the seam flat with a block of wood and a hammer.

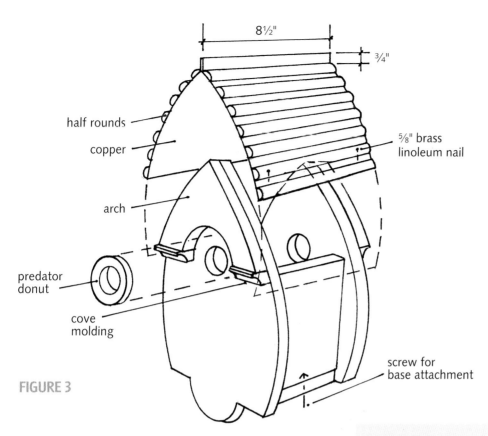

8½"

¾"

half rounds

copper

⅝" brass
linoleum nail

arch

predator
donut

cove
molding

screw for
base attachment

FIGURE 3

10 Spread a thin bead of construction adhesive on the edges of the acorn. Pull the copper sheet firmly over the acorn, allowing it to extend about ½ inch beyond the arch. To hold the shape in place, nail ⅝-inch brass linoleum nails at the ends of the copper sheet, two to each end, as shown in figure 3.

11 With the craft-type backsaw and small miter box, cut fourteen 8 ½-inch pieces from the half-round wood molding. Attach the pieces with construction adhesive and 1-inch brads, nailing the pieces to the edge of the acorn shapes.

12 Reattach the removable base. Countersink all exposed nails and screws. Fill the holes with exterior wood filler and sand smooth.

13 Paint all exposed surfaces with one coat of primer and let dry. Follow with two coats of exterior acrylic latex paint, either in the colors shown or in colors of your choice.

Leaving Enough Space

Cavity nesters, like all birds, require vertical and horizontal space. Most birds are territorial, and during breeding season they all tend to defend areas where the elements of survival can be found, including mates. Bluebirds are particularly territorial and require the right amount of space and the proper habitat. If you want to attract bluebirds to more than one nesting box, place the boxes at least 150 feet apart. Oddly enough, bluebirds will tolerate other species close to their nest boxes—just not other bluebirds.

The size of a territory can vary with the species, population, and competition for suitable nesting places. You will probably not attract more than one pair of each territorial species, but you could have several nesting pairs of different species on your property, all at the same time. You can alter your landscape to provide vertical and horizontal space with well-selected plants and trees, and by providing areas of open space adjacent to planted or forested areas.

Pinstripes

This project is the first of two with a square copper top and a similar Basic Box configuration. In this one, the design's strong lines are created by trim pieces and a paint-combing technique that uses metallic glaze. The paint comb you use has notched edges, each cut with a different-sized groove or tooth. A variety of lines, cross hatches, swirls, and other textures are possible, but for this project we'll keep it simple with traditional pinstripes.

CUTTING LIST

Description	Quantity	Size	Cut From
Front	2	¾ x 5 ½ x 13 ½	1 x 6 pine
Side	2	¾ x 4 ⅛ x 11 ½	1 x 6 pine
Base	1	¾ x 4 x 5 ¼	1 x 6 pine
Trim	2	¼ x ¾ x 8	poplar craft wood

Other Components

Two ¾-inch sections of 3 ½-inch diameter PVC tube, each cut in half

Two predator donuts: 2 ½-inch diameter with 1 ½-inch opening (see page 40)

Instructions

1 Using the metal ruler, combination square, and pencil, lay out the pieces for the fronts, sides, and base along the length of a 1 x 6 board that's 5 feet long. Use the dimensions you see in the cutting list and in figures 1 and 2. Leave enough space between each piece to allow for the saw cut.

2 Use a handsaw for the basic cross cuts, but cut the portions between the front legs with a jigsaw, using pilot starter holes if needed at the corners.

3 Drill the entry holes through the two front pieces—this is a two-sided birdhouse—at the location indicated in figure 1 with a 1 ½-inch spade bit. Drill the air slots through the sides (as also shown in figure 1) with a ½-inch brad- point bit at each end, and then cut the rest of the slot with a jigsaw.

TIP

This project uses two slots for air openings, as the side pieces go all the way to the roof. Its sister project Sponge and Stencil (page 75) avoids the need for slots by leaving the two sides shorter than the top. Really, either way will work fine in either project; the choice is yours.

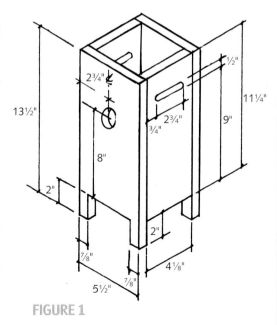

FIGURE 1

Materials

Waterproof exterior glue

6 x 6-inch copper post cap

Exterior wood filler

Medium grade sandpaper

Paint primer/sealer

Exterior acrylic latex paint, satin finish

Metallic copper paint glaze

Acrylic latex caulk

Construction adhesive

Four 1 ¼-inch wood balls

Tools and Accessories

Basic Tool Kit; Power Shop Tools (optional); and Safety Essentials (see page 18)

1 ½-inch spade bit

½-inch brad-point bit

1 ½-inch casing nails

1 ½-inch #8 zinc-coated Phillips-head screws (2)

Hole saw with 1 ½- and 2 ½-inch diameter blades

Finishing nails

4-inch sponge roller or 2-inch-wide paintbrush

Plastic plate

Paint comb with medium-sized notches

4 Attach the fronts to the sides as shown in figure 1, using the glue and 1½-inch casing nails. Use a bench hook or clamps for support. Make sure the top edges of the fronts and sides line up.

5 Position the access base underneath the box to align with the sides. Drill pilot holes through the base on opposite sides for the two #8 Phillips-head screws to temporarily fasten the base for easy removal and maintenance. Do not permanently attach the base.

6 Cut the two predator donuts (see page 40) and the four half-sections of ¾-inch PVC. Try on the copper post cap without attaching it. Then custom cut the two lengths of ¼ x ¾-inch wood stock so that you have two pieces that fit exactly between the tops of the donuts and the roof (about 1 inch long) and two that run from the bottom of the donuts to the middle of the legs (about 7 inches long). Remove the post cap, and set aside the trim and PVC to attach later.

7 Countersink all exposed nails. Fill the holes with exterior wood filler and sand smooth. Prime all exposed surfaces with paint primer and let dry thoroughly.

8 Now you're ready for the pinstripe paint technique. Apply a base coat of bright blue acrylic latex paint with the 2-inch brush or 4-inch sponge roller. Cover all the surfaces you want to pinstripe and let the base coat dry thoroughly.

9 Pour about 2 ounces of metallic copper glaze onto the plastic plate. Apply the metallic glaze over the base coat with the roller or brush. Don't overload the brush/roller or the glaze will run. Using the paint comb, comb from the top to the bottom of the birdhouse in one consistent stroke. To maintain an even pinstripe effect,

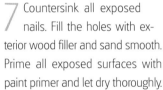

post cap

cap line

¼" × ¾" × 1"

¾" PVC

2½" predator donut

¼" × ¾" × 7"

1¼" ball

base screw

FIGURE 2

5¼"

4"

start the next downward stroke using the last stripe line as your guide. Continue all the way around the box.

10 When the glaze is completely dry, attach the copper post cap by squirting a bead of caulk or construction adhesive around the inner rim of the post cap. Position the cap over the box and press down firmly until it stops. If you press it evenly, the cap should self-align.

11 Paint the predator donuts, wood balls, rim of the post cap, and PVC sections as shown in the project photo or in colors of your choice. Drill pilot holes in all the balls and attach them to the legs with glue and 1½-inch casing nails. Attach the predator donuts, post cap rim, and PVC sections to the surface with construction adhesive. Finally, glue the vertical wood trim into place. If you detached the access base, re-attach it.

Sponge and Stencil

Using some of the same construction techniques as the Pinstripes project, this design combines sponge painting with stenciling. As with that earlier project, you can lay out and cut all the Basic Box pieces from one board, and the birdhouse is crowned with an off-the-shelf copper post cap. The fun part here is adding texture with a sponge and trying your hand at stenciling, using the pattern provided. With a little help from mom or dad, it's a great project for kids on a rainy weekend.

CUTTING LIST

Description	Quantity	Size	Cut From
Front	2	$\frac{3}{4}$ x 5 $\frac{1}{2}$ x 13 $\frac{1}{2}$	1 x 6 pine
Side	2	$\frac{3}{4}$ x 4 $\frac{1}{8}$ x 9 $\frac{1}{2}$	1 x 6 pine
Base	1	$\frac{3}{4}$ x 4 x 5 $\frac{1}{4}$	1 x 6 pine

Other Components

Two predator donuts: 2 $\frac{1}{2}$-inch diameter with 1 $\frac{1}{2}$-inch opening (see page 40)

Instructions

1 On a 1 x 6 board that's 5 feet long, lay out the fronts, sides, and base using the dimensions indicated in figures 1 and 2. Use the metal ruler, carpenter's square, and pencil, and be sure to allow enough space between each piece for the saw cuts.

2 Use a handsaw to cut out the Basic Box pieces and a jigsaw to cut out the space between the front legs. You can use a jigsaw for all your cuts if you prefer.

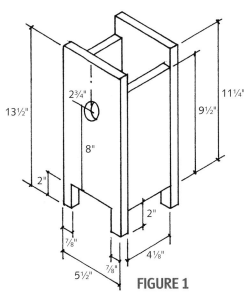

FIGURE 1

3 Using the locations shown in figure 1, drill an entry hole in each front with the 1½-inch spade bit. This is a two-faced birdhouse. Cut two 2 ½-inch predator donuts as explained on page 40.

4 Attach the two fronts to the sides, using glue and 1½-inch casing nails. Make sure you place the sides as shown in figure 1 to allow space for air flow at the top. Use a bench hook or clamps as needed for support.

5 Position the base underneath the box to align with the sides. Drill two pilot holes through the base on opposite sides and the box. Temporarily screw in the two 1½-inch #8 Phillips-head screws. Do not permanently attach the base. The screws allow you to re-move the base for maintenance.

6 Countersink all exposed nails. Fill the holes with exterior wood filler and sand smooth. Paint all exposed surfaces with one coat of paint primer and let it dry thoroughly.

Materials

Waterproof exterior glue
Exterior wood filler
Medium grade sandpaper
Paint primer/sealer
Exterior acrylic latex paint, satin finish
Metallic copper glaze
Stencil material
Stencil spray adhesive
6 x 6-inch copper post cap
1 ¼-inch wood balls (4)
Acrylic latex caulk
Construction adhesive

Tools and Accessories

Basic Tool Kit; Power Shop Tools (optional); and Safety Essentials (see page 18)
1 ½-inch spade bit
Hole saw with 1 ½- and 2 ½-inch blades
1 ½-inch casing nails
1 ½-inch #8 zinc-coated Phillips-head screws (2)
4-inch paint roller or 2-inch-wide paintbrush
Plastic plate
Natural sea sponge
Paper towels
Stencil pattern (see page 125)
Clear plastic sheeting or stencil blank
Craft knife

TIP

When you're doing the sponge paint-ing, you don't want to visually over-power the stencil, but you do want the sponge texture to show. The idea is to strike an even balance.

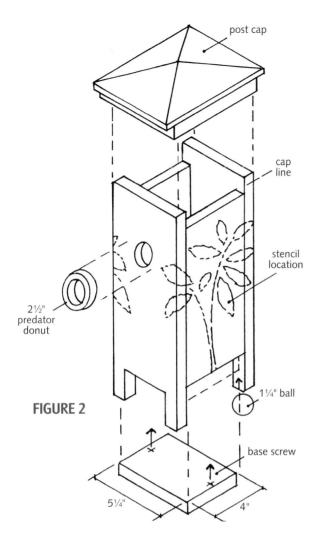

post cap

cap line

stencil location

2½" predator donut

1¼" ball

base screw

FIGURE 2

5¼"

4"

Mix a shade of blue-green exterior acrylic latex paint, darker than the original base color, but not so dark that the stencil design will pop off the surface.

11 Add the copper top by squirting a bead of caulk around the inside rim and placing the top firmly on the box. Press down evenly and the top should self-align.

12 Paint the wood balls, predator guards, base, and post cap rim in a contrasting color (as shown in the project photo or another color you prefer). To fasten the balls to the legs, drill pilot hole in each one and attach them with glue and a 1½-inch casing nail. Attach the predator donuts with construction adhesive. If you detached the access base, re-attach it.

7 Apply a base coat of exterior acrylic latex paint with the brush or sponge roller, in a medium shade of blue/green. Let the base coat dry thoroughly.

8 Pour about 2 ounces of metallic copper glaze onto the plastic plate. Wet the sea sponge with water and wring it out so it's moist but not dripping. Dip the sponge into the glaze, loading it evenly. Lightly dab it on a paper towel to remove any excess glaze. Apply it to a piece of scrap cardboard or paper before beginning on your birdhouse.

9 Apply the glaze in a random fashion to avoid a static, repetitive look, turning the sponge from time to time. Dab some areas a bit more firmly than others to add more color. Cover the entire surface of the box and let it dry thoroughly before continuing.

10 Enlarge the stencil pattern (see page 125) to the size indicated. Follow the stenciling steps described in the sidebar.

Stenciling

I f you plan to use stenciling often in decorating your birdhouses, a number of good books on the topic are available. For the simple stenciling in this project, you only need to follow these steps:

1. Enlarge the design on page 125 to the size indicated.
2. Tape the enlargement down on a level cutting mat and place a piece of clear plastic sheeting or a standard stencil blank securely over the design.
3. Carefully cut the design with a craft-type knife with a sharp, pointed blade.
4. Tape the stencil to your surface, or spray the reverse side with stencil adhesive for flat, even contact.
5. Place a shallow amount of acrylic paint in the bottom of a plastic bowl or plate. Dip a small sponge paint roller in the paint, making sure to test the amount of paint on the roller first to avoid spreading and smearing. Roll over the stencil in one even, smooth stroke.

TIP

Use artist's acrylic, not the type used for household crafts. Artist's acrylic has a richer, fuller body for that one-shot roll.

Paddle House

"Small but versatile" describes this project. With its paddle-type back, you can attach it to a tree, screw it to the side of a house, or surface-mount it to a wood post. This birdhouse is a variation of a 30° gable house, but it features two gables instead of one. The inner gable forms the box; the outer one helps support the roof. Both are functional, but the outer one adds a nice design touch. While assembling this birdhouse is straightforward, make sure you cut all the pieces properly to ensure a neat fit.

CUTTING LIST

Description	Quantity	Size	Cut From
Roof	2	¾ x 7 ¼ x 7 ⅜	1 x 8 pine
Front	1	¾ x 5 ½ x 12 ¼	1 x 6 pine
Back	1	¾ x 5 ½ x 12 ¾	1 x 6 pine
Side	2	¾ x 4 ½ x 7 ½	1 x 6 pine
Base	1	¾ x 5 ¼ x 4 ½	1 x 6 pine
Gable	1	¾ x 3 ½ x 12	1 x 4 pine
Embellishment	1	¼ x ¼ x 10 ½	stock poplar

Materials

Waterproof exterior glue
Acrylic latex caulk
Cove molding
Construction adhesive
Exterior wood filler
Medium grade sandpaper
Paint primer/sealer
Exterior acrylic latex paint, satin finish

Tools and Accessories

Basic Tool Kit; Power Shop Tools
    (optional); and Safety Essentials
    (see page 18)
30° drafting triangle
1 ½-inch spade bit
¾-inch brad-point bit
1 ½-inch casing nails
1 ½-inch #8 zinc-coated Phillips-head
    screws (2)
1 ½-inch trim-head screws
¾-inch brads

Instructions

1 Carefully lay out all the pieces illustrated in figures 1, 2, and 3. Use the metal ruler, carpenter's combination square, and 30° drafting triangle. You can lay out all the pieces (except for the roof sections) on a 1 x 6 board.

TIP

Since a 1 x 6 board actually measures 5 ½ inches wide, it matches the required width of the front and back pieces.

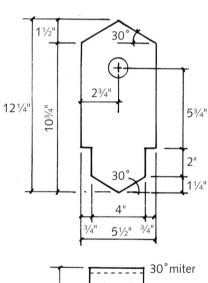

FIGURE 1

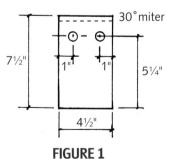

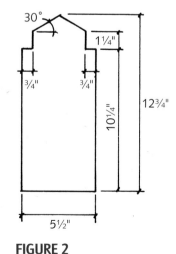

FIGURE 2

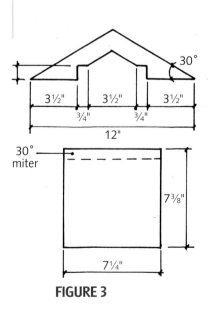

FIGURE 3

2 Make the simple straight-across cuts with a handsaw. Use a jigsaw for the remaining cuts, including your miters.

3 Drill the entry hole as indicated in figure 1 with the 1½-inch spade bit. Note: Unlike most birdhouses in this book, this project has an entry hole in only one front piece. Drill the air holes in each side piece (as also shown in figure 1), with the ¾-inch brad point bit.

4 Attach the front to the sides, one at a time, with glue and 1½ inch casing nails. Make sure the side bevels align with the slope of the front gable so the roof fits properly. Use an adjustable clamp for support if needed. To attach the back, lay the front piece face down on a flat surface. Leaving a ¾-inch space at the bottom for the base (see figure 4), spread glue on the ends of the two sides. Nail the back to each side with 1½-inch casing nails.

5 Set the base under the box so it aligns with the sides. Drill two pilot holes on opposite sides of the base, about ⅜ inch from the edge. These holes are for the 1½-inch #8 Phillips-head screws that will allow you to detach the base for maintenance.

6 Fasten the front outer gable to the box with 1½-inch casing nails and glue. Make sure the two gables align as indicated in figure 4.

7 Attach one roof section at a time. Make sure the bevel of the first section is directly in line with the peak. Spread a bead of caulk along the side edge of the roof section where it meets the back piece. Glue along the beveled edge of the side and gable slopes. Fasten the roof to the side and to the gables with 1½-inch casing nails. Screw the back to the roof section from behind with 1½-inch trim-head screws to draw it up tight against the caulk. Wipe any excess caulk, and then repeat this step for the other roof section.

8 For the gable trim, you will need a section of cove molding at least 15 inches long. You will need to miter two pieces of equal length to join at the peak. Use the small miter box and craft-type back saw to make the miter cuts. Glue and nail each piece—using ¾-inch brads—to the gable end, flush with the roof edge.

9 Again using the craft-type back saw and small miter box, cut seven 1½-inch front embellishments from ¼-inch square stock. Starting ½ inch in from the edge of the front piece, glue each piece to the surface with construction adhesive, allowing a ⅜-inch space between each piece. As a guide, you can draw a light horizontal pencil line 1⅛ inch down the bottom of the outer gable.

10 Countersink all visible nail and screws. Fill with exterior wood filler and sand smooth.

11 Apply one coat of primer to all exposed surfaces and let dry. Paint the project in the colors shown or in colors of your choice, with two coats of exterior acrylic latex paint.

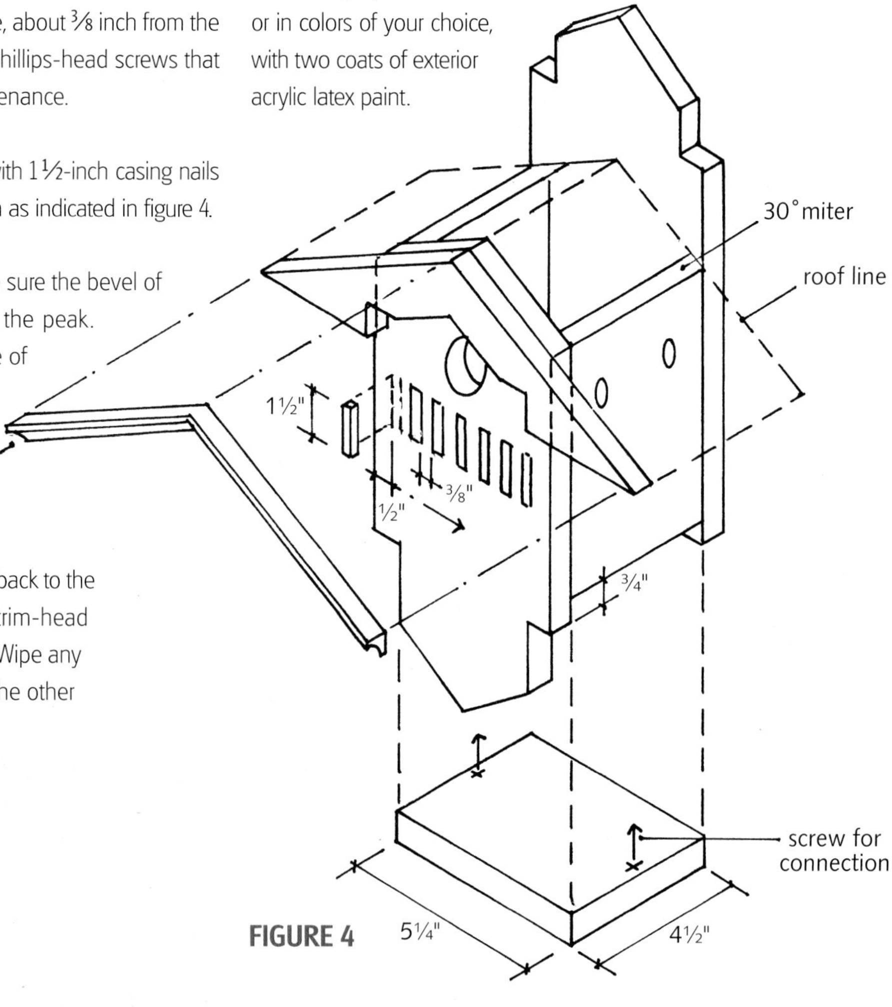

30° miter

roof line

1½"

⅜"

½"

¾"

cove molding

screw for connection

FIGURE 4   5¼"   4½"

Fish or Fowl

S ome people think this project looks like a fish. Others say it's a bird. While I can see the similarities, I assure you I intended neither fish nor fowl. It's just how the creative process operates; you never know what's floating around in the subconscious mind and how it will look once you let it out. This project may have a complicated appearance, but it's actually quite simple to make. The unique part is the bendable plywood that makes this imagined shape a reality.

CUTTING LIST

Description	Quantity	Size	Cut From
Side	2	¾ x 6 ½ x 11	1 x 8 pine
Free form	2	¾ x 6 x 17	1 x 8 pine
Base	1	¾ x 6 x 6 ¾	1 x 8 pine
Front	1	1 x 5 ½ x 11	1 x 6 pine
Back	1	⅜ x 9 x 24	bendable plywood
Trim	1	¼ x ¼ x 36	poplar stock

Instructions

1 Enlarge the freeform template (see page 124) to the size indicated onto heavyweight paper or card stock. Cut out the template with the scissors or craft knife.

2 Tape the template to a 1 x 8 board; use only a piece or two of tape. Carefully trace around the template with a soft pencil. Make a small hole in the center of the cross hair with a nail to locate the entry hole. You will need two identical shapes, so you can either trace the template twice or use the first piece you cut to trace the second. Either way, cut both shapes with a jigsaw.

3 Lay out the three box pieces and the access base, using the metal ruler and carpenter's combination square.

4 Cut the box pieces with a handsaw or jigsaw. Drill the air holes in the front piece (as shown in figure 1) with the ½-inch brad point bit. Drill the entry holes in the free form shapes with the 1½-inch spade drill. If your 24-inch length of plywood is wider than required (9 inches), cut it to the proper width with the jigsaw.

5 Use the paper template to trace the curve required on the two side pieces of the box and to locate the duplicate entry holes. Figure 2 shows the alignment of the free form for tracing the shape. Cut carefully along the traced lines with a jigsaw. Where you marked the cross hair on each side piece, drill entry holes with a 1½-inch spade bit. These holes should line up with those in the freeform piece.

6 Assemble the Basic Box, noting the ⅜-inch front setback (see figure 1). Use glue and 1½-inch casing nails or trim-head screws to fasten the pieces. For support, use the clamps, or a bench hook if you have one.

7 Now attach the freeform pieces. Line up the entry holes and the curve, which should leave a 1¼-inch setback on the side piece.

Materials

Waterproof exterior glue
Exterior wood filler
Medium grade sandpaper
Paint primer/sealer
Exterior acrylic latex paint

Tools and Accessories

Basic Tool Kit; Power Shop Tools (optional); and Safety Essentials (see page 18)
Scissors or craft knife
½-inch brad-point bit
1 ½-inch spade bit
1 ½-inch casing nails
1 ½-inch trim-head screws
18-inch squeeze-type clamps (2)
½-inch brads
1 ½-inch #8 zinc-coated Phillips-head screws (2)

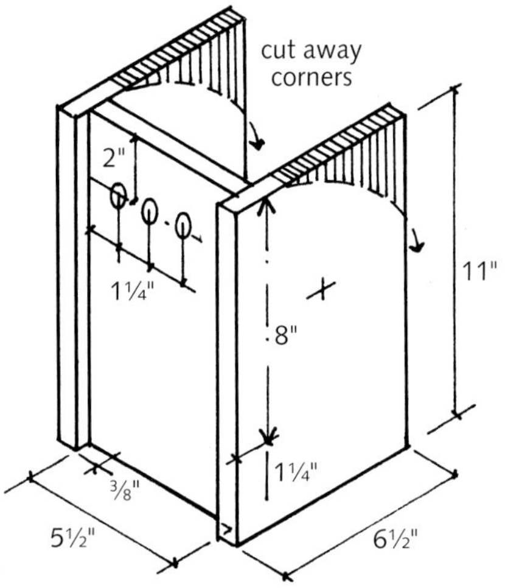

cut away corners
2"
1¼"
8"
1¼"
⅜"
5½"
6½"
11"

FIGURE 1

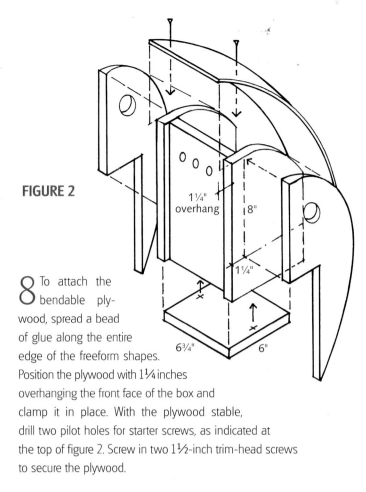

FIGURE 2

1¼"
overhang

8"

1¼"

6¾"

6"

8 To attach the bendable plywood, spread a bead of glue along the entire edge of the freeform shapes. Position the plywood with 1¼ inches overhanging the front face of the box and clamp it in place. With the plywood stable, drill two pilot holes for starter screws, as indicated at the top of figure 2. Screw in two 1½-inch trim-head screws to secure the plywood.

9 Firmly press the plywood to the curved surface. Every two inches along the entire length of the curve, fasten the plywood with 1½-inch trim-head screws. To steady the project while attaching the screws, lay it face down on a flat surface.

10 Now add the ¼-inch square trim pieces, as shown in the project photo. The exact location is somewhat arbitrary. Use the photo as your guide. Attach the trim with ½-inch brads and glue.

11 Position the access base under the box so it aligns with the sides. Drill a pilot hole in opposite edges of the base for the two 1½-inch #8 Phillips-head screws. You can easily remove these screws for maintenance and mounting. Do not permanently attach the base to the box.

12 Countersink all exposed nails and screws. Fill the holes with exterior wood filler and sand smooth.

13 Prime all exposed surfaces and let dry. Follow with two coats of exterior acrylic latex paint in the colors shown or in colors of your choice.

Birds and Their Habitats

Habitat is the natural environment where a species lives and breeds. To survive in the wild, all species require food, water, space, and cover. If your property doesn't have these ingredients already, you will have to create them in order to attract the right birds to your nest box. A man-made environment cannot take the place of one found in nature, but you can create enough diversity to satisfy these essential ingredients for survival.

As a first step, take an inventory of your property to determine what trees and plants you already have, and what needs to be added, removed, or improved upon. A good idea is to make a simple sketch that identifies the primary elements of your landscape, including your house, decks, driveway, and other prominent features. If you're adding to your landscape, remember that what you plant and where you plant it are both equally important. Birds favor areas where different habitats come together, like open areas bordered by trees, or other contrasting edges. Natural settings with loose edges, brambles, and thickets, or gardens where leaves are left to mulch are also effective for attracting birds. Many gardens are too pristine and manicured to serve as habitats for birds, and we are left to wonder why they go elsewhere to nest.

Mix and Match

Sometimes the best designs come from throwing a bunch of things together to see what happens.
This project mixes pieces cut from off-the-shelf chair rail molding with parts hand cut from standard stock.
Together, everything somehow matches, with each piece complementing the other to enrich the surface of an
otherwise ordinary box. The special gable design organizes the ensemble, setting a framework that directs the
placement and size of each added embellishment.

CUTTING LIST

Description	Quantity	Size	Cut From
Roof	2	¾ x 10 x 10	1 x 12 pine
Base	1	¾ x 7 ¾ x 7 ¼	1 x 8 pine
Front	2	¾ x 7 x 7	1 x 8 pine
Gable	2	¾ x 6 ½ x 8	1 x 8 pine
Trim	4	¼ x ¼ x 48	stock poplar
Triangles	2	¼ x 1 x 2	stock poplar
Triangles	12	¼ x 1 x 1	stock poplar
Dowels	8	½ x 2 ½	stock poplar
Flat trim (front)	2	¼ x ⅝ x 8 ¼	stock poplar
Flat trim (side)	2	¼ x ⅝ x 5	stock poplar

Other Components

Predator guard: ¾-inch section of a 3 ½-inch PVC tube

#2, #3, and #6 chair rail pieces (see page 38)

Finial #11 (see page 43)

Instructions

1 Lay out the Basic Box pieces, gables, roof sections, and base using the carpenter's combination square, metal ruler, and 45° drafting triangle. See the cutting list and figures 1, 2, and 3 for measurements.

2 Cut all the pieces, including the gables, with a handsaw or jigsaw. Cut the miters and chamfers with a jigsaw to get the best accuracy. After you cut out the basic gable shapes, drill out the arch using the hole saw with the 2 ½-inch blade. Then cut the 45° slopes as shown in figure 2 to complete the gables.

3 This is a two-faced house, so drill the entry holes in both fronts with the 1 ½-inch spade bit. Then drill the side air holes as shown in figure 1 with the ½-inch brad bit.

4 To assemble the Basic Box as configured in figure 1, use adjustable clamps or a bench hook for support. Spread glue on the edges of the side pieces and attach the fronts to the sides with 1 ½-inch casing nails.

Materials

Waterproof exterior glue
Construction adhesive
1 ¼-inch diameter wood half-balls (2)
Exterior wood filler
Medium grade sandpaper
Paint primer/sealer
Exterior acrylic latex paint, satin finish

Tools and Accessories

Basic Tool Kit; Power Shop Tools (optional); and Safety Essentials (see page 18)
Hole saw with a 2 ½-inch blade
1 ½-inch spade bit
½-inch brad-point bit
1 ½-inch casing nails
½- and 1-inch brads
1 ½-inch #8 zinc-coated Phillips-head screws (2)

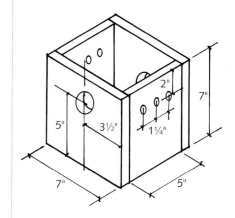

FIGURE 1

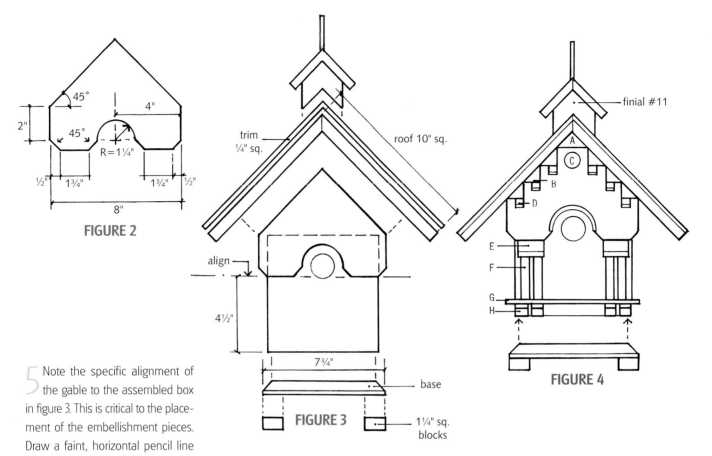

FIGURE 2

45°

2"

45°

4"

R=1¼"

½" 1¾" 1¾" ½"

8"

trim
¼" sq.

roof 10" sq.

align

4½"

7¾"

base

FIGURE 3

1¼" sq.
blocks

finial #11

A

C

B

D

E

F

G
H

FIGURE 4

5 Note the specific alignment of the gable to the assembled box in figure 3. This is critical to the place-ment of the embellishment pieces. Draw a faint, horizontal pencil line 4 ½ inches up from the bottom of the box. Spread glue on the back-side of the gable and attach it to the box with 1½-inch casing nails, using the pencil line as a guiding line. Repeat for the second gable.

6 Set the roof one section at a time. Apply glue to the gable slopes and make sure the roof overhangs the front face of the gable by 1 inch. Attach it with 1½-inch casing nails. Repeat for the second roof section, making a tight miter joint at the peak with glue and casing nails.

7 Add the four 1¼-inch blocks to the base with construction adhe-sive and set the base aside for now.

8 Cut two triangles 1 x 2 inches wide from ¼-inch poplar for the front peak and for the guideline for the others to follow (see fig-ure 4, piece A). Use a backsaw and small miter box. Cut twelve 1 x 1-inch triangles also from ¼-inch poplar (see figure 4, piece B).

9 Following the pattern shown in figure 4, align and glue one 1 x 2-inch triangle at the peak and six 1 x 1-inch triangles, three to a gable, with construction adhesive. Add the 1 ¼-inch half-ball (figure 4, piece C) directly under the 1 x 2-inch triangle, also with construction adhesive (see the project photo for placement). Cut the ¾-inch PVC

section as explained on page 38 and attach it with construction ad-hesive. Repeat to finish the other front.

10 Cut all the chair rail pieces as shown in figure 4—#6 rail is piece D; #2 rail is piece E, and #1 rail is piece H—with the backsaw and miter box. Each will be ¾ inch wide. Cut the dowels (piece F) to the size indicated in the cutting list, but leave the ¼-inch flat trim (piece G) until later.

11 Starting from the gable down, fasten the chair rail pieces in place as shown with construction adhesive. Directly below the #2 chair rail pieces, glue and nail the dowels using 1-inch brads—two to each dowel—leaving a ⅛-inch space between each set (see figure 4). Repeat for the other front.

12 Referring to the cutting list, cut the two flat trim pieces to the size shown for the fronts, and then cut the two flat trim side pieces. The flat trim pieces will form a continuous band around the box directly below the ½-inch dowels (piece G on figure 4). Make sure they fit before you attach them. Then use 1-inch brads and glue to set them in place. If the wood starts to split, use ¹⁄₁₆-inch pilot holes to receive the nails.

WHITEWASH. If you prefer, you can finish your birdhouse in just one color, as with this version of the Mix and Match.

13 Directly below the continuous flat trim strip, attach the #1 chair rail pieces, starting at the outside edge of the box and working inward, leaving a 1/8-inch space between each piece to match the placement of the dowels. Attach the pieces with construction adhesive.

14 Turn the house upside down. Align the base with the box and drill two pilot holes in the base, one each on opposite sides at about 3/8 inch from the edge. These holes are for the 1½-inch #8 Phillips-head screws. The screws make the base easily removable for maintenance. Do not glue the access base to the box.

15 Add the ¼-inch square trim to the ends of the roof as indicated in figure 3. Construct finial #11 (see page 43 for measurements). Locate it at the center point on the roof and glue it in place using the waterproof exterior glue.

16 Countersink all exposed nails and fill the holes with exterior wood filler. Sand the surface smooth. Paint all exposed surfaces with one coat of paint primer. Let dry. Follow with two coats of exterior acrylic latex paint in the colors shown or in colors of your choice.

Providing Nesting Materials

When placing your birdhouse, it's a nice gesture to provide nesting materials nearby. For a bird, building a nest is an arduous and time-consuming task. Here are just some of the materials birds may make use of:

- Small twigs
- Strips of cloth, 1 by 6 inches long
- Feathers
- Pine needles or long grasses
- Yarn and thread, no longer than 4 inches in length
- Cotton pieces
- Dried leaves
- Lint from your dryer
- Strips of cellophane

Place these materials in a very accessible place, like an onion bag hanging from a tree, or an open box resting on a windowsill. Some birds will use anything they find to build their nest. In one reported case, a cavity-nesting titmouse plucked a couple of hairs off a person's head and used them in its nest.

Your Choice

The panel layout of this project suggests how you can create your own design with one simple shape. It's your choice whether to build this project as illustrated or have some fun and innovate. Browse arts-and-crafts shops for a vast array of wood parts, toy parts, game pieces, stars, hearts, nautical shapes, animals, and other ready-made wooden items you can incorporate in your own personal design.

CUTTING LIST

Description	Quantity	Size	Cut From
Roof	2	¾ x 7 ½ x 9 ¼	1 x 10 pine
Base	1	¾ x 7 ¾ x 7 ¾	1 x 10 pine
Front	2	¾ x 6 ½ x 10 ½	1 x 8 pine
Trim bar	2	½ x ⅝ x 9	scrap pine
Blocks	4	¾ x 1¼ x 1¼	scrap pine
L-trim	16	½ x 1¾ x 1¾	16-inch strip, poplar
Entry-hole guard	2	¾ x 3 x 4	scrap pine

Other Components

Finial #12 (see page 43)

Instructions

1 You can lay out the basic pieces for the entire project on one 1 x 10 board that's 4 feet long, using the scrap for the remaining pieces. All you need is the 45° drafting triangle and metal ruler. Follow the dimensions given in figures 1 and 3, and the rest should be easy.

2 Cut all the pieces, even the miter and chamfers on the base. Use a jigsaw for easier cutting, but a handsaw works too. Cut the entry-hole predator guards (see figure 2) and finial (see page 43 for dimensions) as well.

3 This is a two-faced box. Drill entry holes in each front with the 1 ½-inch spade bit and the air holes with a ½-inch brad point bit (see figure 1).

4 Assemble the box by fastening the fronts to the sides with glue and 1½-inch casing nails, as shown in figure 3. Use a bench hook or clamps for support.

5 Now attach the roof, one section at a time, with glue and 1½-inch casing nails. Allow each piece to overhang the front surface by 1⅜ inches. Repeat for the second roof section. Make a tight joint at the peak, using only glue.

Materials

Waterproof exterior glue
Construction adhesive
Exterior wood filler
Medium grade sandpaper
Paint primer/sealer
Exterior latex paint, satin finish
1¼-inch wood half-ball (2), for the finial

Tools and Accessories

Basic Tool Kit; Power Shop Tools
(optional); and Safety Essentials
(see page 18)
1½-inch spade bit
½-inch brad-point bit
1½-inch casing nails
1-inch brads
1½-inch #8 zinc-coated Phillips-head
screws (2)

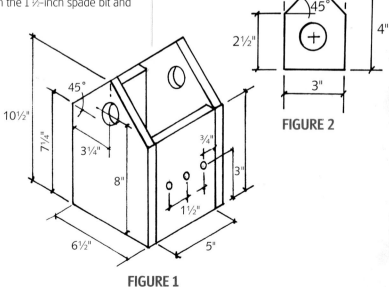

FIGURE 2

FIGURE 1

6 Over each entry hole, glue and nail the entry hole predator guard with 1½-inch casing nails. Directly below it, fasten the trim bar so it touches the sloped roof on both sides. Use glue and 1-inch brads to attach it. The panel beneath the trim is for your pattern.

7 From scrap wood, cut the four 1¼-inch blocks and attach them to the bottom of the base with construction adhesive (see figure 3). Position the base beneath the box so it aligns with the sides. Turn the box upside down and drill pilot holes through the base on opposite sides, at about ³⁄₈ inch from the edge. Temporarily attach the base with the two 1½-inch #8 Phillips-head screws. Do not glue the base to the box; you'll need to remove it occasionally for maintenance.

8 It's "Your Choice" how you create the design on the two fronts. You can fabricate the L-shaped pieces as shown in figure 3 from ½-inch thick poplar (16 pieces in all, 8 for each front), or you can find ready-made pieces to suit your taste.

9 If you decide on ready-made pieces, keep them simple. The challenge is to create a design with just one shape. Whatever you decide, I suggest that you paint the blank panel first and then add the pieces with construction adhesive.

10 Countersink all visible nails. Fill the holes with exterior wood filler and sand the filled holes smooth. Apply one coat of paint primer. Let dry. Follow with two coats of exterior acrylic latex paint in the colors shown or in colors of your choice.

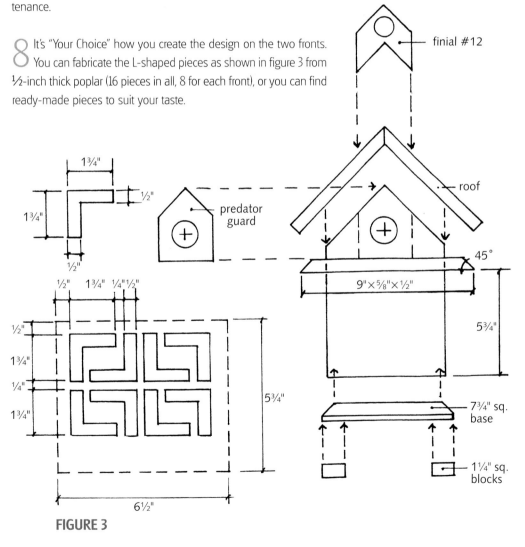

FIGURE 3

Sticks and Blocks

This project uses sticks and blocks to create a design theme that embellishes a Basic Box with 30° integral gables. The sticks are ¼-inch, ready-made poplar strips purchased from a home improvement store. The blocks are hand cut and drilled using simple tools. The feet, added to the legs, are 1-inch wooden thread spools. What pulls the design together is the way ¼-inch bands connect the two fronts and engage only one side; it adds a touch of the unexpected.

CUTTING LIST

Description	Quantity	Size	Cut From
Front	2	¾ x 6 ½ x 15 ½	1 x 8 pine
Side	2	¾ x 6 ½ x 11	1 x 8 pine
Base	1	¾ x 6 x 6 ½	1 x 8 pine
Roof	2	¾ x 4 x 8	1 x 6 pine
Air hole covers	6	¼ x 1¼ x 1¼	poplar flat stock
Trim	3	¼ x ¼ x 36	poplar strips

Other Components

Predator guard, 2 ½-inch square with a 1½-inch entry hole (see page 40)

Finial #2 (see page 42)

4 thread spools, ⅞ x 1 ⅛ inch (available at craft stores)

Materials

Waterproof exterior glue
Acrylic latex caulk
Paint primer/sealer
Exterior acrylic latex paint, satin finish
Construction adhesive
Exterior wood filler
Medium grade sandpaper

Tools and Accessories

Basic Tool Kit; Power Shop Tools
    (optional); and Safety Essentials
    (see page 18)
1 ½-inch spade bit
½-inch brad-point bit
1 ½-inch casing nails
1 ½-inch #8 zinc-coated Phillips-head
    screws (2)
¾-inch brads

Instructions

1 To lay out the pieces, follow the dimensions given in the cutting list and in diagrams 1 and 2. Notice that the two fronts have identical dimensions, but the position of the entry hole and trim are reversed so the front bands join those on the sides. Lay out the pieces with a carpenter's combination square, 30° drafting triangle, and a metal ruler. Don't lay out the ¼-inch trim yet.

2 You can cut the fronts and sides with a handsaw or table saw. Cut the space between the front legs with a jigsaw. Cut the air hole covers (piece A in figure 1) from ¼-inch poplar with a craft-type backsaw and small miter box. Don't cut the bands of ¼-inch square trim until later; it's best to custom cut these pieces as you fit them. Lay out and cut the entry hole predator guards and finial #2.

3 Refer to the roof section of figure 1 for the multiple 30° cuts required for the roof to join at the peak and fit flush with the sides. Use a table saw if you have one. Otherwise, make these cuts very carefully with a jigsaw from a larger-than-required piece of wood so you can clamp it to a solid work surface.

4 Drill the front entry holes and those in the predator guards (see figure 1, piece B) with the 1½-inch spade bit. Drill the air holes and the holes in the center of the air hole covers (piece A) with the ½-inch brad-point bit.

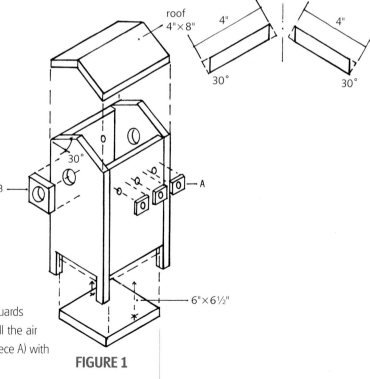

FIGURE 1

5 Assemble the box two pieces at a time. Glue one front to one side as shown in figure 1. Nail the two pieces together with 1½-inch casing nails. Repeat for the second front and side. After you've joined the two halves, center the base under the sides and drill two pilot holes, one each on opposite sides, about ⅜ inch from the edge. Attach the base temporarily to the box with the 1½-inch #8 Phillips-head screws. This connection allows you to remove the base easily for maintenance.

6 Next, attach the roof sections, one at a time, to the gable and sides with glue and 1½-inch casing nails. Before you attach the second roof section, apply a bead of caulk along the peak for a watertight connection. After you've attached the roof, spread a thin layer of caulking over the exposed grain at the roof's edge on both sides.

7 Fasten the air hole covers over the ½-inch holes with glue and ¾-inch brads. Attach the predator guards with glue and 1½-inch casing nails. With the carpenter's combination square, make sure the guards are straight and level; they determine all the trim dimensions.

8 Before adding the trim, paint the box and the finial. Apply one coat of paint primer to all exposed surfaces and let dry. Paint two coats of the color scheme as illustrated in the project photo with the exterior acrylic latex in a satin finish. You may also choose your own colors.

9 Review the dimensions provided in figure 2; then cut and attach the ¼-inch square trim. First attach the continuous piece at the gable line, followed by a vertical and then horizontal piece, custom cutting and fastening as you progress around the box. Fasten the pieces with glue and ¾-inch brads. Don't spread glue over your painted surface. Also, be careful not to split the trim. Use a small tack hammer if you have one.

10 Center finial #2 at the mid-point of the roof and attach with construction adhesive. Then attach the wooden thread spools to the legs the same way.

11 Countersink all exposed nails and fill with exterior wood filler. Sand the wood filler smooth. Then paint the trim and let it dry completely.

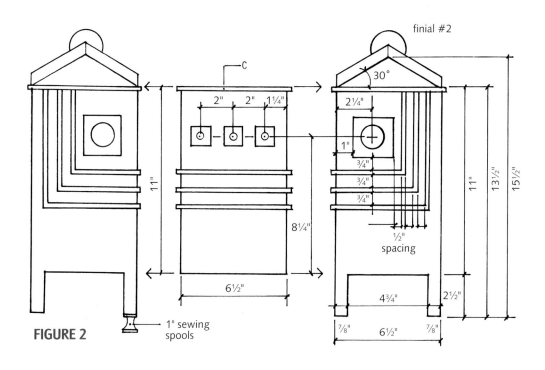

FIGURE 2

Keyhole House

This birdhouse reminds me of a keyhole. Maybe it's the front trim over the entry hole—reminiscent of a "Do Not Disturb" sign—that brings a keyhole to mind. The project is unique in one respect: it's the only one in the book that has two roofs—one on top and one on the side. The keyhole house grew out of the three-sided box structure, but ended up with only two sides and a removable base.

CUTTING LIST

Description	Quantity	Size	Cut From
Front	2	¾ x 7 ½ x 9 ¼	1 x 10 pine
Base	1	¾ x 6 ½ x 7 ½	1 x 10 pine
Roof	2	¾ x 7 ¼ x 8	1 x 8 pine
Side	2	¾ x 1¾ x 5	scrap pine
Blocks	4	¾ x 1¼ x 1¼	scrap pine
Entry-hole guard	2	¼ x 2 ¼ x 4	stock poplar

Other Components

One half of a 3½-inch PVC tube, 8 inches long

M2 molding (see page 39)

Instructions

1 You can lay out the pieces for this entire project on one 1 x 10 board that's four feet long, using the compass, metal ruler, 45° drafting triangle, and carpenter's combination square. Follow the dimensions provided in figures 1 and 2.

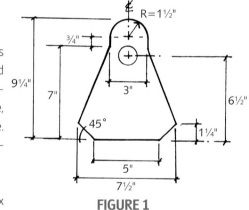

FIGURE 1

2 For the front, start with the 7½ x 9¼-inch rectangle in a vertical (portrait) orientation. Draw a faint pencil line down the center and another 1½ inches to either side, establishing the 3-inch-wide dimension shown in figure 1. Draw two horizontal lines, one 1¼ inches up from the bottom and another 7 inches up. Establish a point 1¼ inches in from each side of the bottom. Draw a line at a 45° angle that intersects the lower horizontal line at the edge of the board (see figure 1). From that point, draw another line on an angle to the intersection of the 7-inch horizontal line and the 3-inch vertical line on the same side. Repeat for the other side to establish the slope for each side roof. See figure 1 to finish the layout, marking the crosshair points for drilling the entry hole. Draw the top half circle with the compass to complete the front shape.

Materials

Waterproof exterior glue

Medium grade sandpaper

Half-round molding

Construction adhesive

Acrylic latex caulk

Exterior wood filler

Paint primer/sealer

Exterior acrylic latex paint, satin finish

Tools and Accessories

Basic Tool Kit; Power Shop Tools (optional); and Safety Essentials (see page 18)

Drawing compass

1 ½-inch spade bit

1 ½-inch casing nails

1 ½-inch #8 zinc-coated Phillips-head screws (2)

¾-inch brads

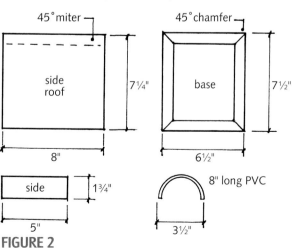

FIGURE 2

With the relatively complicated layout of the fronts, this is a particularly good project for using the front piece you cut first as a template for the second.

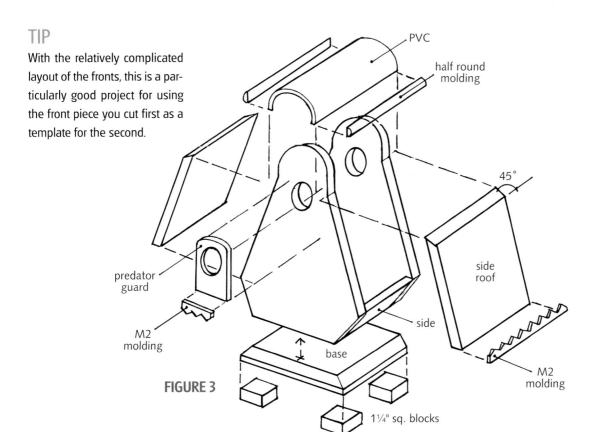

FIGURE 3

PVC
half round molding
45°
side roof
predator guard
M2 molding
side
base
M2 molding
1¼" sq. blocks

3 Cut the straight-edged pieces with the handsaw or jigsaw. To cut the chamfer on the base, use the jigsaw. You can cut the front piece with the jigsaw (or a scroll saw if you have one). Then drill the entry hole in each front using the 1½-inch spade bit.

4 To assemble the box, glue and nail the two small side pieces to the front pieces using 1½-inch casing nails, aligning the sides with the bottom of the box and the sloped front (see figure 3).

5 Add the roof sections with glue and 1½-inch casing nails. Make sure the angled ends align with the bottom pieces (see figure 3).

6 Cut the PVC section in half, and sand any rough edges. Cut two 8-inch lengths of half-round molding and glue them to each edge of the PVC using construction adhesive. To attach the PVC roof, spread a bead of caulk along the curved top of each front piece. Allowing a ¾-inch overhang on both sides, press the PVC firmly on the curved top (see figure 3). Make sure it sits level.

Displaying Your Birdhouses

The process of making something like a birdhouse goes beyond just worrying about functional requirements and sound building techniques. It encompasses the need we all have for beauty and contentment. And with your creation you also play a role in providing for the continued survival of a number of species, and that should make you proud.

You can share your creation with others by placing your handiwork outdoors as part of a garden sculpture, using it as a focal point, or including it as a piece of a well-thought-out ensemble. In your home, a birdhouse can become part of a treasured collection, an interior decoration, or a valued work of art. Regardless of how they are displayed, birdhouses never fail to capture our attention or prompt a smile. No matter how they are fashioned, they are a delight to the eye and a product of the imagination, feeding our fascination for all things small, earthy, and intimate— a sense of home within us all.

7 Complete the base by adding the four 1¼-inch corner blocks with construction adhesive. Set the base under the box and align it with the front pieces. Turn the box over and drill two pilot holes through the base on opposite sides, about ⅜ inch from the edge. These holes are for the 1½-inch #8 Phillips-head screws, and they will allow you to easily remove the base for maintenance.

8 Cut out two entry-hole guards from ¼-inch poplar, following the dimensions in figure 4, and drilling a 1½-inch hole where indicated. Create pieces of M2 molding as described on page 39. Attach these pieces with glue and ¾-inch brads.

9 Countersink all exposed nails. Fill the nail holes with exterior wood filler and sand smooth. Apply one coat of primer to all exposed surfaces, including the PVC. Let dry. Follow with two coats of exterior acrylic latex paint in a satin finish in the colors shown or in colors of your choice.

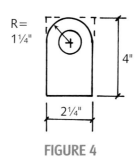

R = 1¼"

4"

2¼"

FIGURE 4

Three for One

Although this birdhouse suits the Eastern and Western Screech Owl, the Northern Flicker and American Kestrel can also use it. It's not uncommon for large species who share similar habitats to use the same size box. You should place 2 to 3 inches of dried leaves in the bottom of the box, because Screech Owls don't gather nesting materials. Screech Owls often start their nocturnal activities 20 to 30 minutes after sunset, so you may never see them. You probably won't hear them either—Screech Owls only screech when agitated.

CUTTING LIST

Description	Quantity	Size	Cut From
Side	2	¾ x 11¼ x 19	1 x 12 pine
Roof	2	¾ x 7⅛ x 11¼	1 x 12 pine
Plateau top	1	¾ x 4 x 11¼	1 x 12 pine
Front	1	¾ x 9¼ x 22¼	1 x 10 pine
Back	1	¾ x 9¼ x 22¼	1 x 10 pine
Base/floor	1	¾ x 9¼ x 10½	1 x 10 pine
Half-circle	1	¼ x 5 x 9¼	flat stock poplar
Entry hole guard	1	¾ x 4 ¾ x 4 ¾	scrap pine

Other Components

2 ¼-inch half-rounds

M1 molding
(see page 39)

Instructions

1 This project might look large and cumbersome, but it's really quite simple. Review figures 1 and 2. Notice that this birdhouse has only one front and that the sides are off-set from the front and back by ⅜ inch. Now lay out the

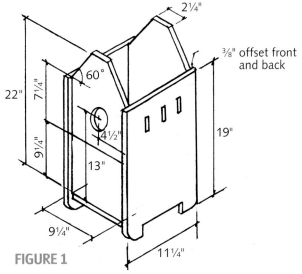

FIGURE 1

Materials

Waterproof exterior glue
Construction adhesive
Exterior wood filler
Medium grade sandpaper
Acrylic latex caulk
Acrylic medium
Paint primer/sealer
Exterior acrylic latex paint, satin finish

Tools and Accessories

Basic Tool Kit; Power Shop Tools
    (optional); and Safety Essentials
    (see page 18)
Metal ruler, 36 inches long
½-inch brad point bit
18-inch adjustable clamps (2)
1 ½-inch trim-head screws
1 ½-inch casing nails
1 ½-inch continuous hinge,
    18 inches long
Metal cutting blade
    (for use with the jigsaw)
½- and ¾-inch brads
2-inch "L" hooks
Scissors or craft knife
Decoupage template (see page 125)

front and back pieces to the same dimensions on a 1 x 10 board. The 1 x 10 board is already the correct width for each piece—9 ¼ inches. Then, lay out the two identical sides on a 1 x 12 board, which is also the exact width required. Cross-cut these four pieces—they do not require ripping. Lay out all the other pieces as indicated in the cutting list and figure 2, using the metal ruler, carpenter's combination square, and 60° triangle.

2 Use the handsaw for all the straight cuts—even the 60° gables. Use the jigsaw to cut out the miters and the space between the legs on the sides. To make the 3-inch entry hole in the front, draw an outline with the compass, drill a starter hole, and then cut out the circle with the jigsaw. Cut the 4 ¾-inch square predator guard the same way, only make sure you use a piece larger than needed so you can clamp it to a solid surface.

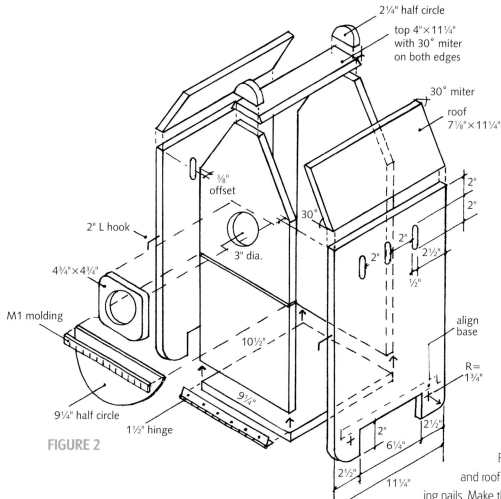

2¼" half circle

top 4"×11¼"
with 30° miter
on both edges

30° miter

roof
7⅛"×11¼"

⅜"
offset

2" L hook

30°

3" dia.

4¾"×4¾"

2"
2"

2"
2"
2½"
½"

M1 molding

align
base

10½"

R=
1¾"

9¼" half circle

9¼"

L

1½" hinge

FIGURE 2

2"
6¼"

2½"

2½"

11¼"

6 Cut the 1 ½-inch continuous hinge into two equal pieces. Use the jigsaw with the metal cutting blade for this. Attach one side to the bottom of the front flap and the other side to the top of the floor using the screws provided with the hinge. The entire front face should now align in one plane.

7 Attach the predator guard with glue and 1½-inch casing nails. Attach the two side roof pieces with glue and 1½-inch casing nails so they align exactly with the sides. Fasten the plateau roof to the gable and roof sections with glue and 1½-inch casing nails. Make the half-rounds as explained on page 37 and attach them to the plateau roof with construction adhesive (see figure 2).

3 The air holes are slots. Drill each end point with the ½-inch brad point bit, and then "connect the dots" with the jigsaw.

4 Lay the sides on a flat surface with the inside up. Draw a vertical line ⅜ inch in from each side edge to establish the location of the front and back offset. Now draw a horizontal line across the front piece 9¼-inches up from its bottom. Cut the piece into two parts and put aside the bottom half for now. This piece is the flap.

5 Spread a bead of glue along the side edges of the back piece and the upper portion of the front. Align the front, back, and two sides as indicated in figure 2. Clamp the four pieces together. Drill pilot holes every 3 inches along the length of the two sides at the front and back intersections and fasten the pieces together with 1½-inch trim-head screws. While the box is still clamped, spread a bead of glue along the bottom of the back piece and on the two sides to attach the floor. Carefully slip the floor piece between the sides so it aligns as shown in figure 1. Nail the floor to the side pieces and the bottom of the back with 1½-inch casing nails.

8 To make the M1 molding, see page 39. Attach the M1 molding to the 9¼-inch half-circle, aligning it exactly along the top edge. Glue and nail the molding in place with ½-inch brads. Next, spread glue evenly over the back side of the half-circle, except for the top ½ inch— but particularly at the other edges. Align the half-circle at the top of the front flap, allowing the top ½ inch to extend above the flap to act as a stop. Nail the half-circle in place with ¾-inch brads. Add the two 2-inch "L" hooks to the edge of the side pieces to engage the flap when it's closed. Once screwed in place, these hooks will hold the flap firmly closed, but you can still unscrew them easily enough to open the box for maintenance.

9 Refer to the sidebar at right for instructions on how to decoupage this birdhouse. A template you can enlarge to make the pattern shown is on page 125. You can affix the enlarged painted design to the half-circle on the front flap. Just follow the directions and embellish as desired.

10 Countersink all the visible screws and nails. Fill the holes with exterior wood filler and sand them smooth. Exposed wood grain will show at the edges of the plateau roof. Spread a thin layer of caulk over the grain to protect it.

11 Apply one coat of paint primer to all the exposed surfaces. Let dry. Follow with two coats of exterior acrylic latex paint in the colors shown or colors of your choice. The box is large, so keep the colors muted.

Decoupage

As with stenciling, you can find more information on decoupage at your local library or craft store. Here's what you'll need for the simple decoupage shown here:

- A pair of scissors

- A small bottle of clear acrylic medium

- Some paper toweling

- A 1½-inch utility brush or a throwaway sponge brush

- A rubber roller (optional)

As a first step, enlarge the design on page 125 on card stock on a copy machine. Next, paint the design directly on the card stock with the illustrated colors or those of your choice. Paint freehand, and don't worry about being precise. Then go back to the copy store to have an exact color copy made of your creation on 24-pound-weight paper; use a digital copier to avoid smearing. Cut out the design and follow these steps to apply it:

1. Prepare the surface you're putting the design on, either by covering it with paint primer or by a single application of clear acrylic medium.

2. Lay the paper reproduction facedown on a piece of wax paper and apply an even coat of acrylic medium, covering the entire design.

3. Pick up the coated paper design and quickly adhere it to the wood surface while the acrylic is wet. Be careful to apply the design accurately, as the medium has a quick grab and set.

4. Once contact is made, press down the design by using a paper towel and working from the middle to the edges. A rubber roller may help to press out any air bubbles. In the event some still remain, prick them with a pin and then press the bubbles down on the surface once more.

5. As a final finish and sealer, apply two to three more coats of clear acrylic medium with a drying period between each coat. Once the acrylic is totally dry, it will withstand the rigors of the outdoors.

Swing Low, Swing Softly

This is the only hanging birdhouse in this book. Why? Most birds shy away from unstable nest boxes. Only wrens will use a hanging box to build a nest and lay their eggs. Male wrens have been known to build preliminary or "dummy" nests in the oddest places—tin cans, hats, shoes, flower pots, and even in pockets of clothing left outdoors. The female chooses one and then proceeds to finish it, sometimes reconstructing it entirely to suit her taste. Wrens are a gardener's favorite since their diet consists mainly of insects.

CUTTING LIST

Description	Quantity	Size	Cut From
Front	2	¾ x 12 x 14	1 x 14 pine
Side	2	¾ x 5 x 5	1 x 6 pine
Base	1	¾ x 5 x 6¼	1 x 6 pine
Gable bar	1	¾ x 1¼ x 5	scrap pine
Aluminum flashing	1	8 x 12 x 21	purchased roll
Entry-hole guard	1	¼ x 3 x 8½	stock poplar

Other Components

Finial #1 (see page 42)

Predator donut (see page 40)

Instructions

1 Lay out the sides and the base to the dimensions indicated in figure 1. Use the metal ruler and carpenter's square.

2 Enlarge figure 3 on heavyweight paper or cardstock to make the indicated dimension 12 inches. Cut the shape out with the craft knife or scissors, and then trace the shape twice onto a board. Mark the crosshairs by making a hole with a small nail at each mark—five in the front and four for the back. This is a one-faced box, so you need only one entry hole.

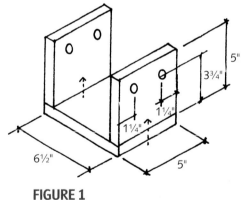

FIGURE 1

3 Cut the freeform shapes (including the entry-hole guard as shown in figure 2) with the jigsaw and the box pieces with the handsaw. Drill the air holes as indicated on figure 1 with a ½-inch brad point bit and the entry hole with the 1½-inch spade bit.

4 Using a small brad point bit (no larger than ⅛ inch), drill holes all the way through the front and back pieces at the crosshair locations. On the backside of each freeform piece, measure 1 inch down from the bottom left and right pilot holes and mark a point (see the template). Connect the dots with a horizontal line. This is where the bottom edge of the two sides will align. Draw a vertical line connecting the top and bottom pilot holes on each side to establish the vertical alignment of the sides.

Materials

Construction adhesive

Waterproof exterior glue

1 ¼-inch wood balls (2)

¾-inch eyelet

Exterior wood filler

Paint primer/sealer

Exterior acrylic latex paint, satin finish

1 ¼-inch diameter wood half-ball

¼-inch dowel, 6 inches long

Tools and Accessories

Basic Tool Kit; Power Shop Tools (optional); and Safety Essentials (see page 18)

Scissors or craft knife

½-inch brad-point bit

1 ½-inch spade bit

Hole saw with 1 ½- and 2 ½-inch blades

1 ½-inch #8 zinc-coated Phillips-head screws (2)

12-inch-wide adjustable clamps (2)

1 ½-inch trim-head screws

⅝-inch brass linoleum nails (4)

¾-inch brads

¼-inch twist bit

1⁄16-inch drill bit

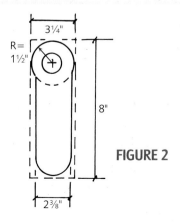

FIGURE 2

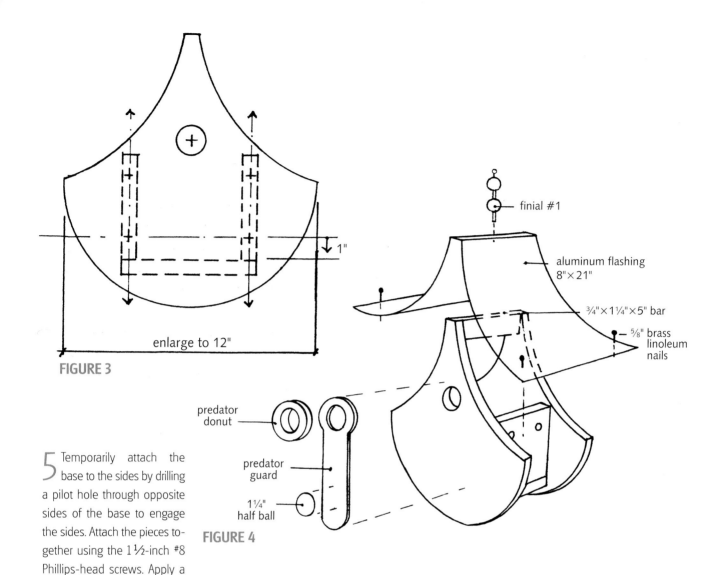

↑1"

enlarge to 12"

FIGURE 3

finial #1

aluminum flashing
8"×21"

¾"×1¼"×5" bar

⅝" brass
linoleum
nails

predator
donut

predator
guard

1¼"
half ball

FIGURE 4

5 Temporarily attach the base to the sides by drilling a pilot hole through opposite sides of the base to engage the sides. Attach the pieces together using the 1½-inch #8 Phillips-head screws. Apply a thin bead of construction adhesive to both edges of each side piece (but not the bottom). Using the location lines that you drew in step 4, press the front and back firmly in line with the sides. Make sure no glue touches the base. Carefully clamp the assembly together and turn it so you can screw 1½-inch trim-head screws through the pilot holes to attach the front and back to the sides.

6 Attach the 5-inch gable bar to the front and back freeform pieces, as shown in figure 4, with glue and a 1½-inch trim-head screw on each side.

7 Cut the piece of aluminum flashing to size, and locate the center point of the length (10½ inches in). Place the flashing over the gable bar at the center point and bend it over the bar using just your hands. It will form a natural crease that matches the ¾-inch width of the bar. When the crease is readily visible, remove the flashing and continue forming the crease by inserting a ¾-inch piece of scrap wood within the crease. You'll find that the flashing begins to form the flare required for attaching it to the freeform shape.

8 Spread a thin bead of construction adhesive along the top of the gable bar and the entire flared edges of the freeform fronts. Allow for a ¾-inch overhang on the front and back, and then press the formed flashing firmly over the freeform. To keep it together, nail a ⅝-inch brass linoleum nail at each end of the flashing (see figure 4).

9 Attach the entry hole predator guard with glue and ¾-inch brads. Attach the predator donut to the predator guard with glue and 1½-inch casing nails.

All about Wrens

There are about 70 species of wrens living in different parts of the world, with the house wren most common to North America. Wrens forage on, or just above, the ground in thick brush, forest, and understory or marsh vegetation. They are friendly around humans and not picky when it comes to nesting. But once a nest site is established, wrens become extremely protective and defensive. They've been known to pester other birds, chasing them from their nests, puncturing their eggs, and even pecking their young to death. They also have been known to destroy other wrens' nests, though why they do it is still unknown.

10 With the ¼-inch twist bit, drill a hole about 1-inch deep at the midpoint of the roof flashing. Squirt construction adhesive in the hole and firmly push the finial #1 into the hole until it stops. With the ¹⁄₁₆-inch bit, drill a pilot hole in the top 1 ¼-inch ball and screw a ¾-inch eyelet into the ball for hanging the box.

11 Countersink all exposed nails and screws. Fill the holes with exterior wood filler and sand smooth. Apply one coat of primer and let dry. Follow with two coats of exterior acrylic latex paint in the colors shown or in colors of your choice.

Roosting Box

Roosting boxes aren't really birdhouses, but they are as necessary to bird survival as nest boxes. During cold, rainy nights or periods of severe weather, small songbirds welcome the refuge a roosting box offers. Birdhouses—due to their limited size; lack of interior perches; and numerous holes for air, drainage, and entry—are unsuitable. A roosting box requires only one entry hole, which allows heat to stay within the box. It's also equipped with staggered interior perches to accommodate more birds, so they can share body heat.

CUTTING LIST

Description	Quantity	Size	Cut From
Front	1	¾ x 11 x 11¼	1 x 12 pine
Back	1	¾ x 11 x 11¼	1 x 12 pine
Side	2	¾ x 6¾ x 10½	1 x 8 pine
Base/floor	1	¾ x 7¾ x 11	1 x 8 pine
Roof	2	¾ x 9½ x 11¼	1 x 12 pine
Mounting brackets	2	¾ x 2 x 3¼	scrap pine
Dowel rod	1	⅜ x 12	stock poplar
Dowels	5	¼ x 4¾	stock poplar
Trim block	1	¾ x 2½ x 2¼	scrap pine
Trim block	1	¾ x 3 x 3	scrap pine
Entry hole predator guard	1	¾ x 3 x 4¼	scrap pine

Other Components

Finial #5 (see page 43)

Instructions

1 The roosting box is a variation of the 45° integral gable box. Using the carpenter's combination square, 45° drafting triangle, and metal rule, lay out the front and back pieces to exactly the same dimensions (see figure 1). Pay particular attention to the back wall with its roosting perches. Next, lay out the sides and base (see figures 1 and 2) to complete the Basic Box.

2 You can cut all the Basic Box pieces, including the 45° angle cuts, with the handsaw or jigsaw. Sand or cut the small curve in the front corner of the side pieces. For each roof section, cut a 45° miter for the peak joint. Draw a line 4 inches down from each miter and cut the roof sections into two pieces along that line (see figure 3). This is where you'll place hinged flaps.

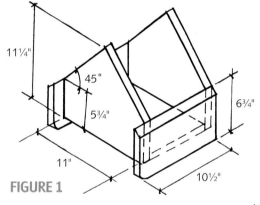

FIGURE 1

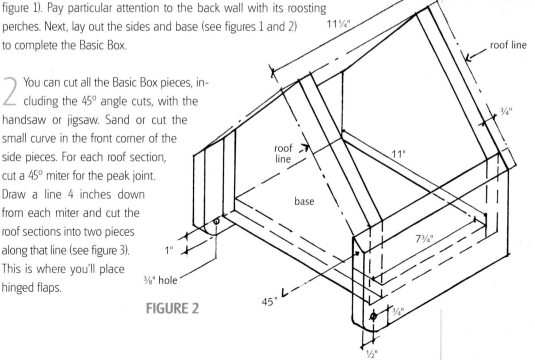

FIGURE 2

Materials

Waterproof exterior glue
Acrylic latex caulk
⅜-inch screw head button
1¼-inch diameter wood half-ball
Construction adhesive
Exterior wood filler
Paint primer/sealer
Exterior acrylic latex paint, satin finish

Tools and Accessories

Basic Tool Kit; Power Shop Tools
    (optional); and Safety Essentials
    (see page 18)
Jigsaw with metal cutting blade
Drawing compass
Hardware cloth, 6 inches square
Household staple gun and staples
1½-inch casing nails
1½-inch trim-head screws
1½-inch continuous hinge,
    24 inches long
1½-inch #8 screws, with button caps (2)
¾- and 1-inch brads
1½-inch spade bit
¼- and ⅜-inch brad-point bits

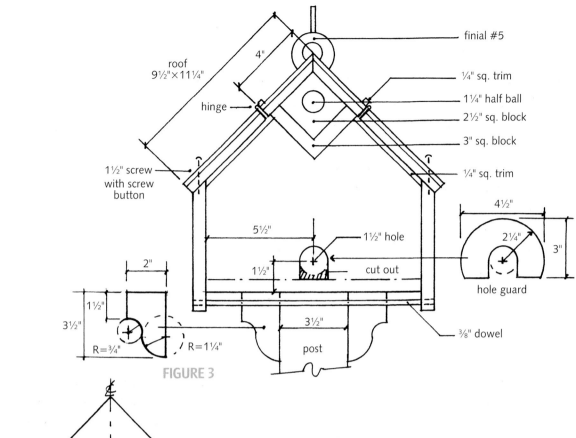

finial #5

roof
9½" × 11¼"

4"

hinge

¼" sq. trim

1¼" half ball

2½" sq. block

3" sq. block

¼" sq. trim

1½" screw
with screw
button

5½"

1½" hole

cut out

1½"

4½"

2¼"

3"

hole guard

2"

1½"

3½"

R=¾"

R=1¼"

3½"

post

⅜" dowel

FIGURE 3

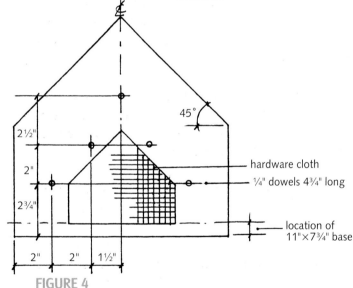

45°

2½"

2"

2¾"

hardware cloth

¼" dowels 4¾" long

location of
11" × 7¾" base

2"   2"   1½"

FIGURE 4

5 To make the roosting perches in the back wall, drill ¼-inch holes, about ⅜ inch deep, at the locations indicated in figure 4. Insert glue in each hole and firmly insert the five ¼-inch dowels. From the hardware cloth, cut a 45° triangle to fit between the perches for the birds to climb on (see figure 4). Attach the cloth with metal staples.

6 Assemble the Basic Box, following figures 1 and 2. Note that the sides are flush with the back piece, align with the sloped gables, and extend beyond the front face. If you cut your pieces properly, they should all fall into place.

3 Drill the entry hole as shown in figure 3, 1½ inches from the bottom of the front piece. Cut out the cross-hatched portion of the diagram below the hole with the jigsaw to complete the entry hole.

4 Finish cutting the larger trim pieces—the 2½- and 3-inch square trim blocks, the mounting brackets, and the hole guard. You'll need the drawing compass to lay out the hole guard, but drill and cut the entry hole as you did for the front piece. The two should match exactly.

7 For this box, you attach the floor to the front and back sections first. Apply glue to the front and back edge of the base/floor, and then nail it together with 1½-inch casing nails. The assembly should sit flush to your work surface. Now attach the sides by aligning the miters with the slope of the gables to form a continuous slope. The sides sit flush against the back and extend beyond the base and front, as shown in figures 1 and 2. Apply glue to the side edges of the gables and the two sides of the base. With 1½-inch trim screws, attach the pieces together to complete the Basic Box (see figure 1).

Why a Roosting Box?

Ever wonder where birds go when nights are cold, the winds are fierce, and snow covers the ground? Some birds have already gone south, but others stay year-round. These birds are called residents. One reported case found 31 winter wrens squeezed into a nest box only 6 inches square.

Normally, songbirds eat constantly during the day and at night fluff their feathers to keep warm. The lucky ones find cavities to roost in, but with natural cavities becoming scarcer, countless birds are lost each year. You can help by building a roosting box such as this one and mounting it in your garden. Mount your box on a pole or post, 4 to 6 feet high, in a sheltered spot facing south, or near dense year-round foliage that can act as a wind buffer. Mount your roosting box within easy reach for cleaning and attach a baffle about 18 inches below the box to ward off unwanted predators.

8. Assemble the roof in sections. Spread a bead of caulking along the mitered edge of one of the 4-inch roof sections. Then attach it to the gable—with glue and 1½-inch casing nails—with its miters at the peak. Use the cut-off roof section to help align the roof with the sides in front, allowing a ¾-inch overhang in back. Repeat to attach the other 4-inch roof section.

9. With the jigsaw and the metal cutting blade, cut the continuous hinge to fit the length of the roof flap (the section that's unattached). Attach each hinge to the flap, making sure the knuckle of the hinge is above the edge of the wood flap or it will bind. Use the screws provided with the hinge. Now attach the other side of the hinge to the fixed 4-inch section of roof. Again, check the spacing of the knuckle. Repeat to attach the second hinge and flap.

10. Drill a pilot hole in each flap to engage the side of the box. Now widen the hole in the flaps to receive the ⅜-inch screw-button cap to prevent rust and predators. Screw in the #8 screws to temporarily close the flaps.

11. With the roof assembled, attach the 3-inch square block on the front directly under the peak with glue and 1½-inch casing nails. Attach the 2½-inch block over the 3-inch one as indicated (see figure 3). Complete the embellishment by centering the 1¼-inch half-ball on the block and fastening it with glue and a 1-inch brad. Over the entry hole, attach the hole guard with glue and 1½-inch casing nails.

12. Drill a ⅜-inch hole in each end of the sides as shown in figure 3 for the ⅜-inch perch dowel. Tap the dowel all the way through both holes until it reaches the outer end of the opposite side. Cut off any excess.

13. Attach the brackets to the underside of the floor with construction adhesive and 1½-inch trim-head screws drilled at an angle to the floor. Leave at least 3½ inches between the brackets so you can mount the box to a post or pole.

14. Construct finial #5 as shown on page 43. Locate the midpoint of the roof and attach it with construction adhesive.

15. Attach the ¼-inch square trim on the roof above the hinge (see figure 3) with glue and ¾-inch brads. Next, attach more of the same trim on the front edge of the gable and on the front face slope immediately below the roof. These trim pieces help to keep out water and wind. Again, glue and nail each trim piece with ¾-inch brads.

16. Countersink all visible nails and screws. Fill the holes with exterior wood filler and sand the holes smooth. Apply one coat of primer to all exposed surfaces. Let dry. Follow with two coats of exterior acrylic latex paint in the colors shown or in colors of your choice.

Features and Patterns

This nest box is the first of three in this book that follows a common theme—change the detail features and you change the look and feel of the design. Triangular gables, with predator guards to match, distinguish this project from the other two. Just a few simple touches like a rich color scheme, overlaid with a pattern of contrasting colors, heighten the interest and add variety to this angular birdhouse.

CUTTING LIST

Description	Quantity	Size	Cut From
Gable	2	¾ x 6 ½ x 6 ½	1 x 8 pine
Front	2	¾ x 6 ½ x 8 ½	1 x 8 pine
Base	1	¾ x 7 ½ x 7 ½	1 x 10 pine
Side	2	¾ x 5 x 6	1 x 6 pine
Blocks	4	¾ x 1¼ x 1¼	scrap pine

Other Components

2 ½-inch square predator guard cut from scrap (2)

Finial #7 (see page 43)

Instructions

1 Lay out the pieces in the cutting list as shown in figures 1 and 2—the fronts, sides, base, and gables—on the requisite boards. Lay out the finial and predator guards on scrap wood. Use the carpenter's combination square, metal ruler, and 45° triangle. This birdhouse is a two-faced box.

2 Cut the Basic Box pieces from figure 1 with the handsaw. Cut the gables, roof miters, and base with the jigsaw. Cut the finial pieces, predator guards, and four wood blocks from scrap. Drill the entry holes as indicated (see figures 1 and 2) with the 1½-inch spade bit. Note that this box does not require air holes.

3 Assemble the box by applying glue to the edge of each side piece and attaching the fronts as shown in figure 3. Fasten with 1½-inch casing nails. For support, use clamps or a bench hook.
Next, spread glue on the backside of one gable where it will encounter the front piece (see figure 3) and attach with 1½-inch trim-head screws or casing nails. Make sure the gable aligns with the top corners of the box exactly as shown in figure 3. Repeat to attach the second gable.

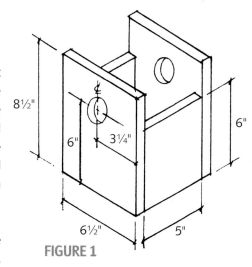

FIGURE 1

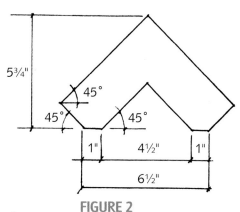

FIGURE 2

6 Locate the midpoint of the roof and attach the finial with construction adhesive. Then attach the predator guards with glue
and 1½-inch casing nails.

7 Countersink all visible nails and screws. Fill the holes with exterior wood filler and sand them smooth.

4 Add one roof section at a time with glue and 1½-inch casing nails. The roof should extend ¾ inch beyond the gable
on both sides. To attach the second roof section, spread a bead
of glue the full length of the miter of the first roof and on the
gable slopes. Press the second section firmly in place and fasten
with 1½-inch casing nails.

5 Attach the four blocks to the underside of the base with
construction adhesive (see figure 3). Set the base under
the box, aligning the sides and fronts
while allowing for the drip edge on the
chamfer. Drill two pilot holes through
the base on opposite sides about ⅜
inch from the edge. Temporarily screw
in the two 1½-inch #8 Phillips-head
screws; they will fasten the base to the
box, but allow you to remove the base
for maintenance.

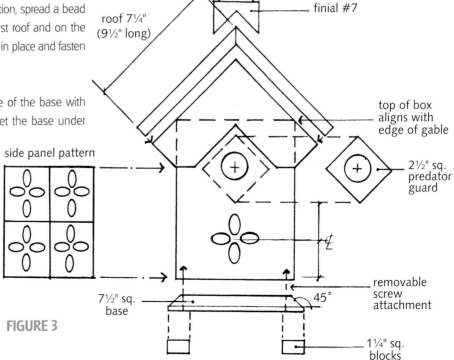

side panel pattern

roof 7¼"
(9½" long)

finial #7

top of box
aligns with
edge of gable

2½" sq.
predator
guard

removable
screw
attachment

45°

7½" sq.
base

1¼" sq.
blocks

FIGURE 3

Maintaining Your Birdhouse

Birdhouses can last for many years and still be serviceable if they are cleaned regularly, repaired as needed, and refinished occasionally to keep the wood from rotting. Some people may like birdhouses with that worn, weathered look, but how would you like to occupy a house with a leaking roof? Some tips to follow for a long-lasting birdhouse:

8 Apply one coat of primer to all exposed surfaces. Let dry. Follow with two coats of exterior acrylic latex paint. When you paint the 5 x 6-inch side panels, you can paint each a different color or alternate the colors within each. Whatever you decide, the squares should differ in color from the main body of the box for variety and interest.

9 While the paint is drying, enlarge the panel design (see the template on page 124) to 5 inches across. Tape it down on a flat surface, protected by a craft mat or sheets of newspaper, and then tape the piece of clear adhesive paper over the design. Do not remove the backing that covers the adhesive portion. With the craft knife, cut out the elliptical shapes within the squares.

10 Carefully remove the adhesive backing from the tracing and press the cutout onto the side panel surface of your birdhouse. Smooth out the design so it adheres flush to the surface. With the sponge roller or soft brush, paint over the cutout. Make sure the roller or brush is not overloaded with paint or it could run or smear. (For more tips on stenciling, see the sidebar on page 77.) Repeat for the other side panel. Make a smaller cutout for the front surface and repeat the process.

1. Nest boxes should be cleaned after each nesting season, or no later than a few weeks before the next one. In the case of wrens and bluebirds, the box needs be cleaned after each brood has gone.

2. For health and safety reasons, wear rubber gloves when removing debris from a nest box. A stiff scrubbing brush, such as an old barbecue grill brush, will help remove any tough grime or bird droppings. If you find parasites or insects, you can clean the inside with a purchased biodegradable, soy-based spray, or make your own spray with one part bleach to nine parts water. Be sure to rinse the inside of the box and let it dry thoroughly before reassembly.

3. The removable base of the birdhouses in this book not only makes cleaning easier, but also allows you to remove the house from its base to store inside during harsh winter weather.

4. As part of your repair program, check for open joints, leaks, rusted hardware or peeling finishes. Replace any spongy wood areas if you can; they'll only worsen over time. If nails have loosened, use screws to strengthen joints and re-caulk any suspect seams.

5. An initial painting job of one prime coat and two finish coats should last a number of years. To maintain a good appearance, clean the outside of your birdhouse regularly to avoid the buildup of harmful mold and mildew.

Pieces and Features

Like the two other projects in this series about changing features, simple geometry plays a key role in altering common elements to change the design. I chose a linear motif for this project, using a square predator guard with a rectangular-cut gable. The linear design is complemented with ¼-inch square strips running vertically on the sides, adding additional color, contrast, and texture. The box is then painted in vivid colors and topped off with an eye-catching finial and brightly colored wood buttons.

CUTTING LIST

Description	Quantity	Size	Cut From
Gable	2	¾ x 6½ x 6½	1 x 8 pine
Front	2	¾ x 6½ x 8½	1 x 8 pine
Base	1	¾ x /½ x 7½	1 x 10 pine
Side	2	¾ x 5 x 6	1 x 6 pine
Blocks	4	¾ x 1¼ x 1¼	scrap pine
Trim	2	¼ x ¼ x 48	stock poplar

Other Components

3-inch square predator guard cut from scrap (2)

Finial #6 (see page 43)

Instructions

1 Lay out the pieces shown in figures 1 and 2—the fronts, sides, base, and gables—on the requisite boards from the cutting list. For the gables, shown in figure 2, a good idea is to make a template on sturdy paper or plastic for tracing the layout (see photo A). Lay out the finial and predator guards on scrap wood. Use the carpenter's combination square, metal ruler, and 45º triangle. This birdhouse, like the others in the series, is a two-faced box.

2 Cut out the Basic Box pieces in figure 1 with the handsaw or saw of your choice. Cut the roof miters, and base with the jigsaw. One way to cut out the gables is to use a table saw with miter gauge (see photo B) and a scroll saw (photo C). You could also use a jigsaw; drilling pilot holes through the inside corners of the cut will make it easier to do it that way. Cut the finial pieces, predator guards, and four wood blocks from scrap. Drill the entry holes as shown in figures 1 and 2 with the 1½-inch spade bit. This box does not re-quire air holes.

Materials

Waterproof glue

Construction adhesive

Exterior wood filler

Medium grade sandpaper

Paint primer/sealer

Exterior acrylic latex paint, satin finish

1-inch wood buttons (4)

Tools and Accessories

Basic Tool Kit; Power Shop Tools (optional); and Safety Essentials (see page 18)

1½-inch spade bit

1½-inch casing nails

1½-inch #8 zinc-coated Phillips-head screws (2)

¾-inch brads

A

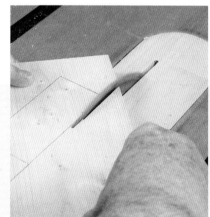

B

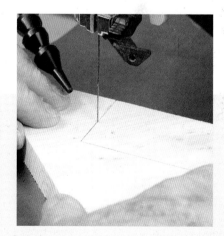

C

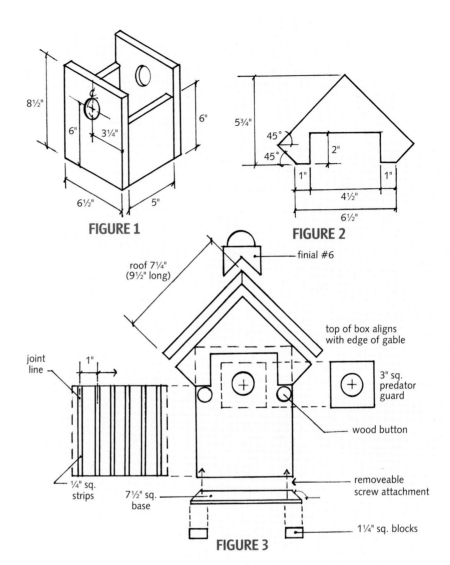

FIGURE 1

8½"
6"
3¼"
6"
6½"
5"

FIGURE 2

5¾"
45°
45°
2"
1"
1"
4½"
6½"

FIGURE 3

roof 7¼"
(9½" long)

finial #6

top of box aligns
with edge of gable

3" sq.
predator
guard

wood button

removeable
screw attachment

1¼" sq. blocks

joint
line

1"

¼" sq.
strips

7½" sq.
base

3 To assemble the box, apply glue to the edges of each side and attach the front pieces as shown in figure 3. Use 1½-inch casing nails to fasten them together, using a bench hook or clamps for support. Next, spread glue on the backside of the gable—but only where it will connect with the front piece—and attach it with 1½-inch trim screws or casing nails. Make sure the gable aligns exactly with the top corners of the box (see figure 3). Repeat for the other gable.

4 Attach one roof section at a time with glue and 1½-inch casing nails. Make sure the roof extends ¾ inch beyond the gable in front and in back. To attach the second roof section, spread a bead of glue the full length of the miter joint of the first section and on the gable slopes. Press the second roof section firmly in place and fasten with 1½-inch casing nails.

5 Glue the four blocks to the underside of the base with construction adhesive. Then set the base under the box so the sides and fronts align, allowing for the drip edge on the chamfer. Drill two pilot holes through the base on opposite sides, about ⅜ inch from the edge to engage the sides. Screw in the two 1½-inch # 8 Phillips-head screws, which will allow you to temporarily fasten the base to the box. You can remove the base easily for maintenance.

6 Attach the finial to the midpoint of the roof with construction adhesive. Then attach the predator guards with glue and 1½-inch casing nails.

7 Cut twelve ¼-inch square trim pieces 6 inches long. You'll need six for each side. Glue and nail the pieces in place with ¾-inch brads as shown in figure 3, spaced 1 inch apart starting from the seam where the front meets the side.

Providing Cover

Birds are cautious by nature and constantly on the lookout for predators. They are extremely alert to movement and sounds, especially during the mating season when their senses are even more attuned to danger. For these reasons birds require cover—areas for an immediate retreat whenever they feel threatened. Dense vegetation—like shrubs, tall grasses, bramble, and trees—acts as cover. Since cover can change with the seasons, you need to consider what grows at different times of the year in order to provide cover year-round. Cover also serves as a roosting place at night and during spells of severe weather. It's especially important to provide cover near a water source, where birds are particularly vulnerable.

8 Countersink all visible nails and screws. Fill the holes with exterior wood filler and sand the holes smooth.

9 Apply one coat of primer to all exposed surfaces. Let dry. Follow with two coats of exterior acrylic latex paint in the desired colors. I recommend contrasting colors for the ¼-inch vertical strips. Follow the color scheme shown in the project photo, or have some fun with using other colors. Keep the colors bright with a lot of contrast.

Features and Stripes

Circular arches, predator guards cut from circles, and a whimsical finial are just a few of the features that separate this project from the two others in the series on changing features. I painted this box in a rich background color, and then I wrapped bright contrasting color bands around it to create visual interest and add a touch of panache. You can follow my color scheme or create your own masterpiece.

CUTTING LIST

Description	Quantity	Size	Cut From
Gable	2	¾ x 6½ x 6½	1 x 8 pine
Front	2	¾ x 6½ x 8½	1 x 8 pine
Base	1	¾ x 7½ x 7½	1 x 10 pine
Side	2	¾ x 5 x 6	1 x 6 pine
Blocks	4	¾ x 1½ x 1½	scrap pine

Other Components

3-inch round predator guard cut from scrap (2) (see page 40)

Finial #8 (see page 43)

Instructions

1 Lay out the pieces shown in figures 1 and 2, including the base, gables, and sides, on the requisite boards from the cutting list. Lay out the predator guards and finial on scrap pieces. This birdhouse, like the others in the series, is a two-faced box.

2 Cut out the Basic Box pieces from figure 1 with a handsaw. Use a jigsaw to cut the gables, roof miters, and base. Cut the finial pieces, predator guards, and four wood blocks from scrap. Drill the entry holes as indicated in figures 1 and 3 with the 1½-inch spade bit. Note that this box does not require you to add air holes.

3 Assemble the box the same way you did the other two projects in this theme: apply glue to the edge of each side and attach the fronts with 1½-inch casing nails (see figure 3). For support, use clamps or a bench hook.

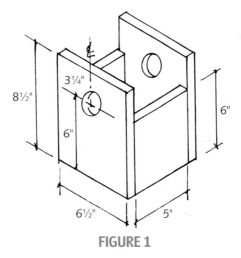

FIGURE 1

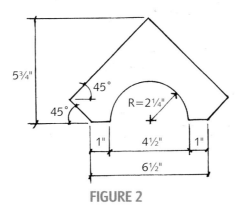

FIGURE 2

Materials

Waterproof glue

Construction adhesive

Exterior wood filler

Medium grade sandpaper

Paint primer/sealer

Exterior acrylic latex paint, satin finish

Painter's masking tape, ½-inch wide

Tools and Accessories

Basic Tool Kit; Power Shop Tools
   (optional); and Safety Essentials
   (see page 18)

1½-inch spade bit

1½-inch casing nails

1½-inch #8 zinc-coated Phillips-head
   screws (2)

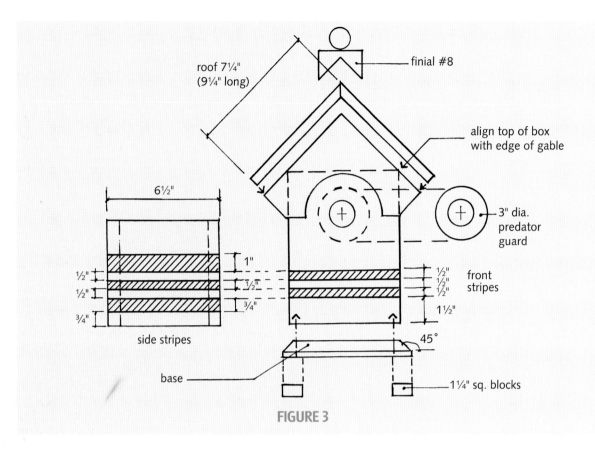

roof 7¼"
(9¼" long)

finial #8

align top of box
with edge of gable

6½"

3" dia.
predator
guard

1"

½"
½"
½"
front
stripes

½"
½"

1"
½"

¾"

¾"

1½"

¾"

side stripes

45°

base

1¼" sq. blocks

FIGURE 3

Next, spread glue on the backside of the gable—but only where it will connect with the front piece—and fasten it with 1½-inch trim screws or casing nails. Make sure the gable aligns with the top corners of the box exactly as shown in figure 3. Repeat to attach the other gable.

4 Making sure the first roof section extends ¾ inch beyond both gables, attach it to the box with glue and 1½-inch casing nails. For the second roof section, spread a bead of glue the full length of the miter of the first section and on the gable slopes. Press the second roof section firmly in place and fasten it with 1½-inch casing nails.

5 Glue the four blocks to the underside of the base with construction adhesive. When it's dry, set the base under the box, aligning the sides and fronts while allowing for the drip edge on the chamfer. Drill two pilot holes through the base on opposite sides about ⅜ inch from the edge. When you screw in the two 1½-inch #8 Phillips-head screws to engage the sides, you'll have a way to temporarily fasten the base to the box, while allowing you to easily remove the base for maintenance.

6 Attach the finial to the midpoint of the roof with construction adhesive. Then attach the predator guards with glue and 1½-inch casing nails.

7 Countersink all visible nails and screws. Fill the holes with exterior wood filler and sand the holes smooth.

8 Apply one coat of primer to all exposed surfaces. Let dry. Follow with two coats of exterior acrylic latex paint. You can try my color scheme or devise one of your own, but keep the colors bright, with a lot of contrast. To achieve the overlaid stripe pattern, tape off the segments with painter's tape as shown in figure 3 and apply two more coats of paint in a contrasting color.

PURELY DECORATIVE. I don't expect birds to take up residence in these three houses I mounted on the side of my house—I didn't even add the predator guards—but they do brighten up a plain brick wall.

Placing Your Nesting Boxes

When you place your box is important for attracting the birds you want. In warm climates, particularly in southern regions, make sure your nest box is placed by February; in northern climates set it out no later than mid- to late-March. Be patient. Birds may not find your box immediately, and it may take a season or two until they feel it's safe to approach it.

Golf courses, open fields, and farms are good places to set out nest boxes, but avoid areas where pesticides and herbicides may be present. Such agents not only harm birds, but they also destroy insects that are essential for a bird's diet.

Some more suggestions for placing your birdhouses:

- For a given species, it's best not to place more than four nest boxes per acre.

- Don't place birdhouses too close to feeders, as all that activity can be disturbing.

- Avoid hanging birdhouses unless you want to attract wrens; the movement doesn't seem to bother them.

- To thwart predators, place your nest box at least 10 feet from trees, houses, fences, or other jumping-off places.

- Don't place your nest box in areas with a lot of disturbance and noise.

- If you have to place your birdhouse near a street or road, face the entry hole away from the roadway to prevent fledglings from meeting with disaster.

- When orienting your nest box: in the north, face the entry south; in the south, face it east or north. In the breeding season you want to avoid the hot summer sun. In cooler climates birds welcome the warmth of the sun.

Templates

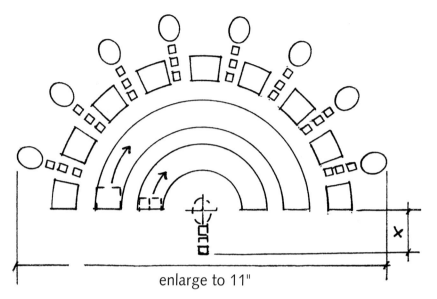

enlarge to 11"

Marbles and Chips, page 52

enlarge to 5"

Features and Patterns, page 110

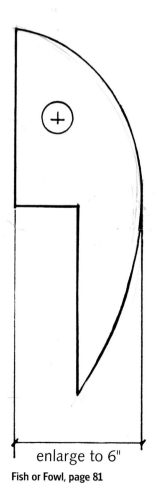

enlarge to 6"

Fish or Fowl, page 81

enlarge to 9¼"

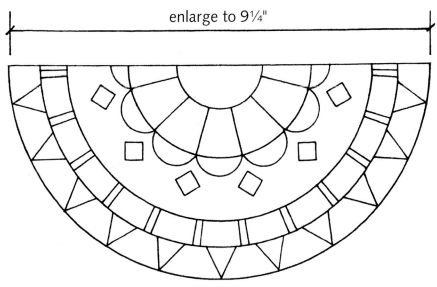

Three for One, page 98

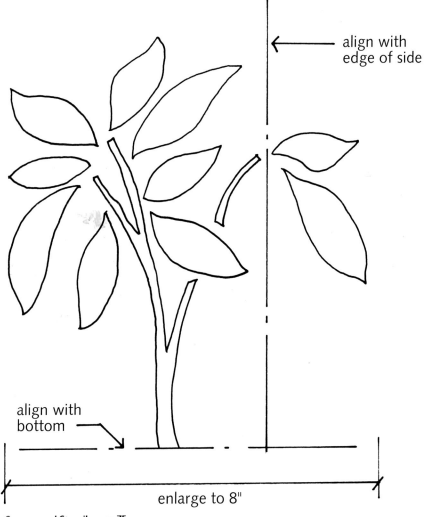

align with
edge of side

align with
bottom

enlarge to 8"

Sponge and Stencil, page 75

Dedication

To my loving wife, Marilyn, for her unwavering patience. Without her faith and support this book would not have been possible.

Special Remembrance . . .

To Mom, who passed away May 30, 2007—three weeks shy of her 102nd birthday.

Acknowledgments

Putting a book together is an arduous task. It requires the joint effort of many people working together, each contributing a special talent. It begins with the author, and is shepherded through the technical process by the editors and other professional staff. The end result is only as good as the team itself, and in this case—it's perfection.

Starting with Carol Taylor, and including the entire staff at Lark Books—thank you. You have made this experience a cherished and memorable one.

I would like to individually thank Terry Krautwurst, my original editor, and Kathy Sheldon, who filled in and was always available for consultation and advice. And a very special word of thanks to Larry Shea, who came in midstream, picked up the pieces, and crafted a seamless work of editorial excellence.

My appreciation and gratitude goes out to art director Susan McBride, cover designer Cindy La Breacht, the editorial and art production assistants at Lark, and the photographers. Through their combined effort, they have taken my words and designs and fashioned a book that rises to a work of art.

Lastly, I would like to thank the thousands upon thousands of birds that enrich our lives with their melodic songs and natural beauty. Without them life would be poorer, and this book would not have been conceived.

Fly away—fly away—fly away home!

Metric Equivalents

Inches	Centimeters		Inches	Centimeters
⅛	3 mm		12	30
¼	6 mm		13	32.5
⅜	9 mm		14	35
½	1.3		15	37.5
⅝	1.6		16	40
¾	1.9		17	42.5
⅞	2.2		18	45
1	2.5		19	47.5
1	3.1		20	50
1	3.8		21	52.5
1	4.4		22	55
2	5		23	57.5
2	6.25		24	60
3	7.5		25	62.5
3	8.8		26	65
4	10		27	67.5
4	11.3		28	70
5	12.5		29	72.5
5	13.8		30	75
6	15		31	77.5
7	17.5		32	80
8	20		33	82.5
9	22.5		34	85
10	25		35	87.5
11	27.5		36	90

Index